Lecture Notes in Computer Science

T0199097

Lecture Notes in Computer Science

Lecture Notes in Computer Science

Edited by G. Goos and J. Hartmanis

119

Graeme Hirst

Anaphora in Natural Language Understanding: A Survey

Springer-Verlag
Berlin Heidelberg New York 1981

Author

Graeme Hirst
Department of Computer Science, Brown University
Providence, RI 02912, USA

AMS Subject Classifications (1970): 68 F 20, 68 F 30, 68 G 99
CR Subject Classifications (1974): 3.42, 3.60

ISBN 3-540-10858-0 Springer-Verlag Berlin Heidelberg New York
ISBN 0-387-10858-0 Springer-Verlag New York Heidelberg Berlin

Printing and binding: Beltz Offsetdruck, Hemsbach/Bergstr.
2145/3140-543210

CONTENTS

In loving memory of my Father

PREFACE

I was a victim of a series of accidents.
*   — Kurt Vonnegut Jr[1]*

This report was started in the boreal summer of 1976, making its first appearance as Hirst (1976b), and was completed almost three years later, after a number of lapses and relapses. Like a chinchilla one is trying to photograph, the field I was trying to describe would not sit still. Therefore, while I have tried to incorporate all the changes that occurred in those years, there may be some blurring at the edges.

I have tried to make this survey comprehensible both to the computer scientist who has no grounding in linguistics, and to the linguist who knows nothing of computers. However, it has been necessary to presume some information, since digressions to explain transformational grammar or Fillmore's case theory, for example, were clearly impractical. (Readers not familiar with these may wish to read an introductory text on transformational grammars such as Jacobsen (1977), Akmajian and Heny (1975) or Grinder and Elgin (1973), and Fillmore's (1968) introduction to cases. The reader not familiar with artificial intelligence will find Winston (1977), Boden (1977) or Bundy (1979) useful introductions.)

It is to be noted, that when any part of this paper
appears dull, there is a design in it.
*   — Richard Steele[2]*

How to read this report

This is a long report, but few people will need to read it all. The Chapter outlines below will help you find the sections of greatest interest to you.

Chapter 1 introduces and motivates work on natural language understanding and in particular anaphora. If you are already motivated, skip to Chapter 2.

---

[1]From: *The sirens of Titan.* London: Coronet, 1967, page 161.

[2]In: *The tatler*, number 38, Thursday 7 July 1709. Reprinted in: *The tatler, with notes and illustrations.* Edinburgh: Robert Martin, 1845, volume 1, page 236.

Chapter 2 defines anaphora formally, and motivates the idea of "conscious-ness" as a repository for antecedents. Section 2.3 is an exposition of the vari-ous types of anaphora. I suggest that readers familiar with anaphora neverthe-less at least skim this section, as I have included a number of unusual examples and counterexamples which are often ignored but which should be considered by anyone claiming to have a complete anaphor-handling system or theory.

Chapter 3 reviews traditional approaches to anaphora resolution, and shows why they are inadequate. Section 3.1 discusses the work of Bobrow, Winograd, Woods and his associates, Schank and his students, Taylor, Hobbs and Wilks. Then in section 3.2 I abstract and evaluate the approaches these people took.

In Chapter 4, I show the importance of discourse theme and anaphoric focus in reference resolution.

In Chapter 5 I review five current discourse-oriented approaches to ana-phora — those of Kantor, Grosz, Sidner, Webber, and the discourse cohesion approach of Lockman and others. Approaches to non-NP anaphora are also out-lined here.

Chapter 6 describes the role of anaphor-specific information in resolution, and integrates theories of causal valence into a more general framework.

Chapter 7 discusses some issues raised in earlier chapters, such as psycho-linguistic testing, and also the problems of anaphora in language generation. The report concludes with a review of outstanding problems.

Copious bibliographic references will keep you busy in the library for hours, and an index of names will help you find out where in this work your favorite work is discussed. A subject index is also provided.

Notation

In the sample texts in this report, I use underlining to indicate the anaphor(s) of interest, the symbol ϕ to explicitly mark the place where an ellipsis occurred, and small capitals to indicate words that are stressed when the sen-tence is spoken. Superscript numbers in parentheses are sometimes used to explicitly label different occurrences of the same word in a text. Variant read-ings of a text are enclosed in braces, with the variations separated by a vertical bar. A sentence which is grammatical but unacceptable in the given context is denoted by "#". As usual, "*" and "?" denote text which is ill-formed and of questionable well-formedness, respectively.

In the main body of the report, I use small capitals for emphasis or to indi-cate that a new term is being defined. Italics have their usual metalinguistic role in referring to words and phrases. *NP* and *VP* stand for *noun phrase* and *verb phrase*.

By *I*, I mean myself, Graeme Hirst, the writer of this document, and by *we*, I mean you, the reader, and me together. So, for example, when I say *I think*..., I am expressing a personal opinion; whereas when I say *we see*..., I am pointing out something about which the reader and I undoubtedly agree — and we don't, the fault is probably in the reader.

PREFACE TO THE SPRINGER EDITION

I originally wrote this report as a thesis for the Master of Science degree in the Department of Engineering Physics, Australian National University. The thesis was also published as technical report 79-2 (May 1979) by the Department of Computer Science, University of British Columbia,

In the year or so preceding the first publication of the report, the study of anaphora in natural language understanding was a very current topic, with the publication of several important doctoral theses (which are reviewed in Chapter 5). I had originally believed that the field was changing so fast that the survey would be substantially out of date within a year. This has not proved to be the case; rather, work in the area has slowed, as researchers pause to evaluate and reconsider the approaches taken. I now think that this report has a longer-than-anticipated life expectancy, and that it will continue to be helpful to those constructing natural language understanding systems.

The present edition was typeset with a text-formatting system that is unfortunately typical of many found in computer science departments, in that it was designed by people who know a lot about computers but not very much about typography or book design. I hope therefore that you will forgive the occasional footnote that runs onto a new page when it shouldn't have, some ludicrous hyphenation, the funny shape of certain letters, and the awkward widows that turn up in a few places. The page numbers in the indexes should be regarded as approximate only, especially where the reference is in a footnote carried over to the next page.

Providence, 1 May 1981

ACKNOWLEDGEMENTS

Who made me the genius I am today —
The mathematician that others all quote?
Who's the professor that made me that way?
The greatest that ever got chalk on his coat!
One man deserves the credit, one man deserves the
    blame,
And Nicolai Ivanovich Lobachevsky is his name.
        — Tom Lehrer[1]

I wrote this survey while a graduate student at the Department of Computer Science, University of British Columbia; my supervisor was Richard Rosenberg. Parts were also written at the Department of Engineering Physics, Research School of Physical Sciences, Australian National University (ANU), under the joint supervision of Stephen Kaneff and Iain Macleod.

Without the encouragement of Robin Stanton, this work would never have been started.

Discussions with and/or comments and criticism from the following people improved the quality of this report: Roger Browse, Wallace Chafe, Jim Davidson, Barbara Grosz, M A K Halliday, Alan Mackworth, Bonnie Nash-Webber (in 1977), Doug Teeple and Bonnie Webber (in 1978). Nevertheless, the mistakes are my responsibility (except in any instance where, in presenting the work of another, I have been misled through the original author's inability to communicate coherently, in which case the original author must take the blame).

Financial support came from the Australian Department of Education as a Commonwealth Postgraduate Research (CPR) Award, from ANU as a CPR Award supplement, and as a special grant from the ANU Department of Engineering Physics.

Many spelling errors and stylistic grossosities have been eliminated through the detective work of Mark Scott Johnson, Nadia Talent, Iain Macleod and M W Peacock.

Finally, I want to especially acknowledge the help of two people: Richard Rosenberg, who first interested me in this work and encouraged me to complete it, and Nadia Talent, without whom it would all have turned out quite differently.

---

[1]From: Nicolai Ivanovich Lobachevsky. On: Lehrer, Tom. *Songs by Tom Lehrer.* LP recording, Reprise RS6216.

Chapter 1

INTRODUCTION

> *I gave her one, they gave him two,*
> *You gave us three or more;*
> *They all returned from him to you,*
> *Though they were mine before.*
> — *Lewis Carroll*[1]

1.1. Natural language understanding

This thesis addresses a problem central to the understanding of natural language by computer.[2] There are two main groups of reasons for wanting a computer to understand natural language: practical and theoretical.

In the set of practical reasons is useful human-machine communication. At present, computer programs, database queries and the like must be expressed in some artificial computer language, human use of which requires training and practice. If people were able to specify their instructions to computers in their own natural language, then they would be able to avail themselves of computer services without the need to learn special languages.

Presently, there are some prototypical systems which answer questions or write programs in response to commands expressed in a subset of English. Of these, few other than LSNLIS (Woods, Kaplan and Nash-Webber 1972) and ROBOT (Harris 1977, 1978) have been tested in the real world of potential users. Each system uses a slightly different subset of English, providing varying coverage and habitability;[3] however, none is without important gaps. For more discussion of this point, and a survey of some systems, see Petrick (1976).

Also of practical use would be a machine translation system which could translate documents from one natural language to another. Some such systems are already in everyday use (Hutchins 1978), but their performance still leaves much to be desired.

The theoretical reasons for studying NLU are to create, test and study models of language. Presently, major models of language such as

---

[1]From: *Alice's Adventures in Wonderland.* Chapter 12.

[2]"Natural language understanding" may be abbreviated "NLU".

[3]The HABITABILITY (Watt 1968) of a subset of English is the ease with which a user can conform

transformational grammars (Chomsky 1957, 1965) and generative semantics (Lakoff 1968, 1971; McCawley 1968; reviewed by Gelbart 1976) have in practice been synthetic rather than analytic; that is, they account for sentence structure by generating the sentence from a DEEP REPRESENTATION.[4] However, this is only one half of the communication process; the other is perceiving and understanding the sentence. So far there has been no equally significant model for this, the analytic component of language. Research into computer programs which understand can help fill this gap. Not only does such research lead in the direction of a model, but implementation as a computer program provides a means for testing and evaluating analytic theories and models; in a sense, the implementation IS the model (cf Winston 1977:258; Weizenbaum 1976:140-153).[5]

In this thesis, we shall be interested in the second reason as much as the first. Therefore, we will, as much as possible, be investigating the whole of a natural language, specifically English, rather than restricting ourselves to a habitable subset for human-machine communication. Further, we shall be considering connected discourse rather than isolated sentences. The motivation for this is that many of the interesting problems of language, such as cohesion and reference, do not occur in their full glorious complexity in a single sentence. (This is not to imply, however, that there are not still problems aplenty in single sentences.)

> *The term anaphora does not appear in many texts and monographs on linguistics, or it appears only in passing — an omission not at all surprising, given the fact that the concept of anaphora is of central importance to discourse structure.*
> — *William O Hendricks (1976:65)*

1.2. Reference and anaphora

The particular problem we shall be considering is that of anaphora and reference. Reference is a central concept in language, and is one that philosophers have studied and pondered for many years (for example, Russell (1905), Strawson (1950), Linsky (1963) and Donnellan (1966)). In recent years, linguists,

---

to its restrictions.

[4]Theoretically, this statement is not correct. Chomsky (1957:48) emphasizes the neutrality in principle of transformational grammars with respect to synthesis or analysis of sentences. In practice, however, transformational grammars have not proved useful in automatic NLU; see section 3.2.5 and Woods (1970:596-597).

[5]I am aware that whether an implementation can constitute a theory is a controversial point, and I do not wish to pursue it here, as it has been discussed at much length in the oral presentations at (but, regrettably, not in the written proceedings of) the second conference on Theoretical Issues in Natural Language Processing, at the University of Illinois at Urbana-Champaign, July 1978. (For a summary of the views expressed at the conference on this matter, see Hirst (1978a).) It is necessary here only to assert the weaker view that an implementation, if not itself a theory, can aid understanding of a theory. Friedman, Moran and Warren's (1978) computer programs for Montague grammars exemplify this.

psychologists and artificial intelligence (AI) workers have seen its relevance to their fields, and have researched many aspects of it.

The problem essentially is that of how words are able to denote concepts, and in particular how a certain sequence of words can denote a unique concept. For example, if I meet you and say, apropos of nothing:

(1-1)   The chinchilla ate my portrait of Richard Nixon last night. It devoured it so fast, I didn't even have a chance to save the frame.

you are somehow able to determine that by *Richard Nixon* I mean Richard Milhous Nixon, ex-President of the United States of America, and not Richard Chomsky Nixon, sanitation engineer of Momence, Illinois. You further understand which chinchilla, of all in the world, I mean by *the chinchilla*,[6] that *it devoured it* refers to the aforementioned chinchilla's aforementioned act of eating the aforementioned portrait, and that *the frame* is the frame of the aforementioned portrait.

Any language comprehender needs to make decisions all the time similar to those you made in reading the last paragraph. It needs to identify concepts when they are initially referenced and to identify subsequent references to them. Loosely speaking − we shall have a more formal definition in the next chapter − ANAPHORA is the phenomenon of subsequent reference.[7]

Because no coherent discourse is without both initial and subsequent reference, it is essential that any (computer) NLU system not limited to single sentence input be able to handle reference. (It is also advisable even in systems so limited, since intrasentential reference is very common.) That is the motivation for this thesis.

---

[6]Note that it is not enough that *the chinchilla* identify the particular chinchilla uniquely to each of us. We must also both know that it identifies the same chinchilla to both of us. It is sometimes necessary that such mutual knowledge regress to infinity to ensure the felicity of such definite references; see Clark and Marshall (1978) for a demonstration of this, and a solution to the problems it raises.

[7]Do not confound this sense of the word *anaphora* with its use in rhetoric to mean the deliberate repetition of a word or phrase at the start of several successive verses or paragraphs, nor with its liturgiological meanings.

1.2 Reference and anaphora

Chapter 2

ANAPHORA

*I shall not attempt to give a serious definition of ana-
phoric element, a task which presupposes an understanding of this aspect of language which is, in my opinion, not now available.*

— *Paul Martin Postal (1969:205)*

*The term "anaphora", used several times above, will not
be determined with any greater precision in this paper
than is usual; and far from reducing the number of
open questions about anaphora, I will actually add to
that number.*

— *William C Watt (1973)*

2.1. What is anaphora?

ANAPHORA[1] is the device of making in discourse[2] an ABBREVIATED reference to
some entity (or entities) in the expectation that the perceiver of the discourse
will be able to disabbreviate the reference and thereby determine the identity
of the entity. The reference is called an ANAPHOR,[3] and the entity to which it
refers is its REFERENT or ANTECEDENT.[4] A reference and its referent are said to be
COREFERENTIAL. The process of determining the referent of an anaphor is called
RESOLUTION. By ABBREVIATED, I mean containing fewer bits of disambiguating
information (in the sense of Shannon and Weaver 1949), rather than lexically or

---

[1]The terminology and many of the basic concepts described in this section are derived from
Halliday and Hasan (1976).

[2]By a DISCOURSE we mean a section of text, either written or spoken, which is COHERENT in
the sense that it forms a unified whole (Halliday and Hasan 1976). We do not restrict its length,
nor do we limit the number of speakers in the conversation in the case of spoken discourse.
For convenience, we will sometimes refer to the speaker and listener of a discourse, using
these terms to subsume respectively the writer and reader of written text.

[3]This term is due to Edes (1968).

[4]Webber (1978a) distinguishes between a referent and an antecedent, calling "antecedent" the
invoking description of which the referent is an instance — see section 5.4. We will not need to
make this distinction, and will follow general usage, using the two terms interchangeably.

phonetically shorter (Hirst 1977a).[5] Note that one possible realization of an anaphor is as a complete void — an ellipsis; see section 2.3.13.

Two simple examples of anaphors are shown in (2-1) and (2-2):

(2-1) Daryel carried a pewter centipede and a box to put <u>it</u> in.

(2-2) Because Nadia was passing the sex shop, <u>she</u> was asked to buy half a kilo of pornography.

Here, *it* and *she* are anaphors with referents *a pewter centipede* and *Nadia*, respectively. In these particular cases, the referents occurred explicitly in the text and did so before the anaphor. Neither need be the case. In the next example, (2-2) is recast with the anaphor first:[6]

(2-3) Because <u>she</u> was passing the sex shop, Nadia was asked to buy half a kilo of pornography.

That the referent need not be explicit is shown in these texts (the first based on an example of Grimes (1975:46), the second, Webber (1978a)):

(2-4) When Ross visited his Aunt Cicely, <u>they</u>[1] spent the afternoon talking. Then, as arranged, Nadia arrived. Ross kissed his aunt goodbye, and set off with Nadia to the discotheque, where <u>they</u> [2] danced the night away.

(2-5) Ross gave each girl a crayon. <u>They</u> used <u>them</u> to draw pictures of Daryel in the bath.

In (2-4), *they*[1] refers to the set {Ross, Aunt Cicely}, and *they*[2] to {Ross, Nadia}. Neither of these sets is mentioned explicitly, and the listener has to piece them together from the explicitly given elements. In particular, the MEANING of the text must be used to obtain the referent of *they*[2]. In (2-5), *they* and *them* are the sets of girls and crayons, respectively, whose existence is inferred from the first sentence.

> *There are no discounts on person-to-person calls. Check your phone book or the inside covers of this directory to see how and when these discounts apply in your area.* [7]

Conversely, an explicitly mentioned entity need not be referable — if negatively quantified, for example:

---

[5]Although most anaphors ARE lexically shorter than their antecedents, we shall later see some that are not.

[6]Strictly speaking, a reference which textually precedes its referent is called a CATAPHOR. Cataphors and anaphors are together called ENDOPHORS (see Halliday and Hasan 1976:14-18, 31-37). Again, we will usually be sloppy, and use the term *anaphor* to refer to both forms of endophor, except where repugnant to the context. Sometimes we will also include exophors (see below in this section).

[7]From an advertisement for the TransCanada Telephone System, 1978.

(2-6) Ross doesn't have a car. #It is a battered old Skoda.

(2-7) Ross doesn't have a car any more. It was completely destroyed in an accident last week.

(2-8) Ross doesn't have a car, and if he did, it probably wouldn't run.

It is unacceptable to predicate anything of the non-existent car in (2-6), but acceptable in (2-7) because the car's previous existence is implied.   In (2-8), *it* refers not to the car Ross doesn't have, but to the one in the expansion of *did* as *did have a car* that he might have.

Often, an anaphor with a non-explicit antecedent refers to something more complex than a set of explicitly mentioned items. Consider these texts:

(2-9) The boy stood on the burning deck
       Picking his nose like mad.
       He rolled it[8] into little balls
       And threw it at his dad.[9]

(2-10) Ross sat in the corner, knitting madly. Suddenly he threw it down, and stormed out of the room.

What was thrown in each case is the PRODUCT of the previously described actions and components, namely the results of the nose-picking and Ross's knitting, respectively.

Sometimes the antecedent is nothing more than something brought to mind by part of the text. Here are some examples:

(2-11) Ross wanted to NAIL the boards together, but Sue made him do it with TAPE

(2-12) Nadia dreams a lot, but seldom remembers them.

(2-13) When I first saw your gallery, I liked the ones of ladies.[10]

(2-14) Idi Amin is a bad joke, unless you are unfortunate enough to live there.[11]

(2-15) Early one morning at the end of August, a truck came up to the house. We loaded the paintings of the summer into the back, and closed and locked the doors. We stood on the porch and watched the truck drive off.
       "He is a careful driver," Jacob Kahn said. "I have used him

---

[8]This usage has been called the DESPICABLE *IT* (Corum 1973).

[9]From: Turner, Ian Alexander Hamilton. *Cinderella dressed in yella: Australian children's playrhymes*. Melbourne: Heinemann Educational, 1969, page 104, rhyme 26116.

[10]From: Mitchell, Joni. The Gallery. On: Mitchell, Joni. *Clouds*. LP recording, Reprise RS6341. The quoted text is the opening lines of this song; not all informants found it completely acceptable.

[11]Not all informants found this sentence completely acceptable.

before."[12]

(2-16) Nadia wants to climb Mt Everest, and Ross wants to tour Africa, but neither of them will ϕ because they are both too poor.

(2-17) Ross and Nadia wanted to dance together, but Nadia's mother said she couldn't ϕ.

In (2-11) (due to Watt 1973:466) the referent of *do it* is clearly *fasten the boards together*, though this is only implied by the verb *nail*.[13] In (2-12) (which is due to Corum (1973)), *them* refers to Nadia's dreams. In (2-13), *ones* refers to the pictures brought to mind by the mention of the gallery. In (2-14) the referent *Uganda* for *there* is suggested by mention of Amin. Similarly, in (2-15), the arrival of the truck suggests the presence of the driver, and this is enough for him/her[14] to be referenced anaphorically. In (2-16) (from Webber 1978a), the elided verb phrase *do what she/he wants to do* is a single VP combining and abstracting its two antecedents *climb Mt Everest* and *tour Africa*, and in (2-17) (also from Webber 1978a), the ellipsis stands for *dance with Ross*.

EXOPHORS[15] refer deictically (Fillmore 1972) (that is, in a pointing manner) to items in the external world rather than in the text. For example, in (2-18):

(2-18) Pick that up and put it over there.

that and *there* are exophors whose referent in the real world is something that the situation, perhaps including physical pointing, makes clear to the perceiver of the text.

In summary, an anaphor is a reference whose antecedent is a concept or entity EVOKED implicitly or explicitly by the preceding text or situation.

2.2. Anaphors as references to entities in consciousness

In the previous section I described an anaphor as a reference that "the perceiver of the discourse will be able to disabbreviate". I now wish to elaborate

---

[12]From: Potok, Chaim. *My name is Asher Lev*. [1] Penguin, 1973, page 231. [2] Heinemann, 1972.

[13]Watt (1973) has called this phenomenon — verbs like *nail* which can have related concepts extracted from them as antecedents — PENETRABLE REEFS (cf Corum 1973).

[14]Most people sexistly assume the truck driver to be male, and hence find (i) jarring in the same context:

(i) "She is a careful driver," Jacob Kahn said.

[15]The term *pragmatic anaphora* has been used for exophora by Hankamer and Sag (1976), and picked up by several other authors. The term is misleading, and will not be used here, as almost ALL anaphora is, in a sense, pragmatic (cf Morgan 1978; Partee 1978).

on this, and to qualify it.[16]

The qualification is to the words "will be able", which might better be "is expected by the speaker to be able". For when a speaker uses an anaphor, there is no iron-clad guarantee that the listener will in fact have the ability to resolve it. For example, the listener may have been busy thinking about something else and didn't even hear the referent of the anaphor; or, more frequently, the referent was mentioned so far back in the discourse that the listener has completely forgotten it, as (2-19) demonstrates:

> (2-19) Just as Carrie, played by Sissy Spacek, can be seen as another of De Palma's ambiguous women, as in *Obsession*, other parallels in the construction of the two films spring rapidly to mind. One can compare, for example, the extraordinary power of the final moments of the present film, in which the gentle, sunlit, Vaseline-lensed scene is shattered by a sudden horror that makes many people literally jump out of their seats, with that of *Obsession*, wherein the unexpected again happens, though this time in the negative sense that the expected does not happen.
>
> However, despite De Palma's skill, it is <u>her</u> acting that ultimately makes the film.

Here, few people, especially those not familiar with the films being discussed, would be able to resolve *her* as Sissy Spacek without consciously looking back through the text to find the referent. Anyone who didn't know that De Palma is male might have erroneously chosen him as the antecedent.

What is illustrated here is this: for an anaphor to be resolvable, its antecedent must be in what we shall for the time being call the listener's "CONSCIOUSNESS".[17] When a speaker uses an anaphor, they assume (usually correctly) that its antecedent is in the listener's consciousness and is therefore resolvable; if they are wrong, the discourse becomes ill-formed from the listener's point of view. Chafe (1970) has likened consciousness to a stage. Mentioning a concept, even implicitly, puts it on stage, from where it slowly retreats into the wings unless mentioned again. Concepts can be referenced anaphorically when and only when they are on stage (subject always to the constraints of syntax).

The speaker's assumption is apparently based on a model of the listener's consciousness which the speaker maintains (cf Winograd 1976). There have been no investigations into the nature of this model (but see Norman, Rumelhart and the LNR Research Group (1975:68ff) and Grosz (1977a, 1977b)), nor even has its psychological reality ever been shown. It is, however, probably part of a larger model of the listener that the speaker constructs, the necessity of which has been shown by Cohen and Perrault (1976), Perrault and Cohen (1977), and Cohen (1978), to mention but a few (cf also Webber (1978a)).

---

[16]The influence of Chafe (1972, 1974) and Nash-Webber and Reiter (1977) is evident in this section.

[17]For readability, I will not in future put the quote marks round *consciousness*. However, they should be understood as intended whenever I use the word. In section 3.2.1 I introduce better terminology.

2.2 Anaphors as references to entities in consciousness

How does an antecedent enter the listener's consciousness in the first place? There are four basic ways. The first, illustrated by examples (2-1) and (2-2), is that the antecedent be explicitly mentioned in the text, and further, as we have just seen, this mention must be "recent".[18]

The second is similar, except that the mentioning is implicit. We saw this in example (2-4), where things like set elements were given, causing the listener to be "conscious" of the set itself. Again "recency" is relevant.

The third and fourth ways antecedents may enter consciousness result in exophors when the entity is referenced. We saw the third illustrated by (2-18), a sentence which would be accompanied by pointing (or a similar gesture) to draw the listener's attention to what *that* is and where *there* is.

The fourth method is qualitatively different from the other three, in that the speaker does not deliberately cause the antecedent to enter the listener's consciousness. Instead, the speaker makes a calculated guess that other means have previously placed it there. Here is an example: The scene is a party at a wealthy person's home, and one of the guests is admiring a painting on the wall. The host comes up and says:

(2-20) Do you like it? It's an original Chagall.

The host can use *it* to refer to the painting because it is clearly the upper-most thing on the guest's mind at that moment − or at least so the host assumes. If in fact the guest was merely staring blankly into space in front of the painting, the guest would probably not realize at first what the host was talking about.

It follows from the above that if a computer is to take the part of a listener in discourse, it too must have a consciousness, or a model thereof, to understand anaphora. Further, if it is to generate discourse, it must make judgements about its listener's consciousness to use anaphora correctly; that is, it will need to model its hearer's consciousness. In this thesis we will be primarily concerned with the former case, namely modelling a listener's consciousness on a computer for anaphora resolution.

> *Anaone,*
> *Anatwo,*
> *Anathree,*
> *Anaphor!*
> − *Mark Scott Johnson*[19]

---

[18]Much of this thesis will be concerned with determining exactly what is meant here by *recent*.

[19]Personal communication.

2.2 Anaphors as references to entities in consciousness

2.3. Varieties of anaphora

Before you can resolve an anaphor, you have to know that it's an anaphor. This section, therefore, will be devoted to identifying the common or garden varieties of anaphora, and also a few more exotic species.[20]

2.3.1. Pronominal reference

The word *pronoun* has two meanings. Firstly, it can refer to a part of speech such as *he*, *she*, *it*, *they* or *that*. Secondly, it can refer to an anaphor whose antecedent is a noun phrase, that is one which "stands in place of a noun". In classical grammar, these meanings were generally taken to be equivalent. However, we shall see that they are not, and there are many cases in which pronouns in the first sense are not pronouns in the second sense, and vice versa. In this thesis, we shall generally use the word *pronoun* with its first meaning. To avoid confusion, we shall say that pronouns in the second sense of the word are PRONOMINALLY REFERENT.

Most pronouns ARE pronominally referent. For example:

(2-21) Ross bought {a radiometer | three kilograms of after-dinner mints} and gave {it | them} to Nadia for her birthday.

(2-22) Nadia wanted a gold ring, but Ross bought her a plastic one.

(2-23) Ross told Nadia about the coming of the Antichrist. It is due very soon, and he has bought exclusive film rights to it from the Vatican.

Pronouns are usually marked for gender and/or number, which is often useful in resolution. However, there are awkward exceptions. In this text, *she* refers to a person, film director Robert Bresson, who is probably marked as male in the listener's world knowledge:

(2-24) Who is this Bresson? Is she a woman?[21]

Similarly, in the novel *Even cowgirls get the blues*[22] the character named The Countess is introduced on page 63. It is not until page 66 that we find out that The Countess is male, and we are told this only implicitly by the author's referring to him by the pronoun *he* when there is no other possible referent. A human reader is momentarily fazed by this, but finds recovery easy.

---

[20]This section is an expansion of a similar section in Hirst (1976b). An alternative taxonomy appears in Nash-Webber (1977) and Webber (1978a).

[21]From: Robinson, David. Festival report: Berlin. *American Film*, *III*(1), October 1977, 68-70, page 68.

[22]Robbins, Tom. *Even cowgirls get the blues*. New York: Bantam, 1977.

A similar problem, which is becoming increasingly common, is the use of the SINGULAR EPICENE pronoun — a genderless plural third-person pronoun referring to a singular third-person of unknown, or deliberately unmarked, gender. For example:[23]

(2-25) %The author thanks the reader for their kind indulgence.

(2-26) %The most important qualification for the new programmer I want to hire is that they be fluent in Cobol.

(2-27) "Would it not be possible for someone to come out by way of the drawing-room window and in this one while Mr Fitzroy was out of the room, and return the same way?" [asked Poirot.]
%"But we'd have seen them," objected the Admiral.[24]

(2-28) %Neither Ross nor Sue sank their teeth into my apple.

((2-28) is based on an example from Whitley (1978:19).) In many idiolects, these uses of *their*, *they* and *them* are acceptable substitutes for *his/her*, *he/she* (sometimes rendered as *s/he*) and *him/her*. Other idiolects fiercely reject such laxness in selectional restrictions, and such idiolects may be an unstated reason why some people virulently oppose current moves to "desex" language. A computer NLU system should be willing to give people the benefit of the doubt in this respect, and thus be able to understand text like the above examples, even though an occasional ambiguity may be thereby engendered.[25] For more discussion on the use of the singular epicene *they*, see Whitley (1978).

The horrible bureaucratese expression *same* acts like a pronoun with the special restriction that it can only refer to very recent noun phrases, usually the one immediately preceding it:

(2-29) Persons using this coffee urn must clean same after use.

(2-30) Complete the enclosed form and post same to the above address.

Interposing another noun phrase, *he/she* and *black ink* in the following examples, makes the sentence very marginal, at least in my idiolect:

(2-31) ?When the user has finished with this coffee urn, he/she must clean same.

(2-32) ?Complete the enclosed form in black ink and post same to the above address.

Intersentential reference with *same* also reduces acceptability:

---

[23]The symbol "%" indicates a sentence whose acceptability varies widely over different idiolects.

[24]From: Christie, Agatha. The submarine plans. in: *Poirot's early cases*, Fontana/Collins, 1974, page 130. [This text was originally published some time between 1923 and 1936.]

[25]The astute reader will have already noticed that this thesis is written in the lax idiolect.

(2-33) ?Complete the enclosed form. Post <u>same</u> to the above address.

2.3.2. Pronominal noun phrases: Surface count anaphors

Certain noun phrases also act as pronominal anaphors. These include *the former* and *the latter*. We shall call these SURFACE COUNT ANAPHORS:

(2-34) Sue stared at the pumpkin and the turnip, and declared that she preferred <u>the former</u>.

(2-35) One union, Prince Rupert Co-op Fisherman's Guild, owns a fish processing plant there. The other, the Amalgamated Shoreworkers and Clerks Union, represents workers in the plant. <u>The former</u> locked out <u>the latter</u> on June 23 when they couldn't agree on a contract for the workers.[26]

The former example suggests that ordinal numbers can also be construed as anaphors, as in (2-36):

(2-36) Nadia removed from her bag a tissue, a dime and a crumpled dollar note, and absentmindedly handed the cashier <u>the first</u> instead of <u>the third</u>.

Although not great literary usage, this is syntactically correct and we understand its meaning. (See also Postal (1976).)

Surface count anaphors require not only that the antecedent be in consciousness, but also that the surface structure of the sentence (or at least the order of possible referents) be retained. This leads to the problem of what a possible referent for such an anaphor is. For example, (2-36) contains six noun phrases before *the first*; you probably didn't notice that there were so many, let alone count them. They are: *Nadia, her bag, a dirty tissue, a dime, a crumpled dollar note* and *the cashier*. (There is also an elided seventh, *Nadia*, before *absentmindedly*.) If *the first* and *the third* simply counted NPs in the sentence, their referents would be, respectively, *Nadia* and *a dirty tissue*, though we understand them unambiguously to be *a dirty tissue* and *a crumpled dollar note*. Clearly, to resolve such anaphors computationally, we need some way of knowing where to start counting.[27]

---

[26]From: Evans-Atkinson, Evan. From your side: Labor dispute causes waste of good fish. *The Vancouver sun*, 11 July 1978, page B6.

[27]One often sees sentences like (i) or, even worse, (ii) and (iii) in sloppy writing:

(i) ?Ross was carrying a large box. <u>The latter</u> was brown.

(ii) ??Ross entered the room with a box under his arm, and put <u>the latter</u> on the mantelpiece.

(iii) ??We know well that potent insect Xylocopilpil, which is to the Xylocopid as the auk to

If there are too many items to be counted in a text with a surface count anaphor, the result is unacceptable, as not all possible referents can be retained in consciousness at once:

(2-37) On the twelfth day of Christmas my true love gave me eight ladies dancing, six drummers drumming, eleven songbirds singing, nine pipers piping, fifty lords a-leaping, seven federal agents, a swarm of swans a-swimming, five pogo sticks, four cauliflowers, three french fries, two cans of yeast and a parsnip in a pear tree. #I returned all but the eleventh to the store the following morning.

2.3.3. Pronominal noun phrases: Epithets

Epithets can also be used pronominally, as in these texts:

(2-38) Ross used his Bankcard so much, the poor guy had to declare bankruptcy.

(2-39) When John found out about Mary's marital infidelity, the bastard punched her.[28]

Lakoff (1976) has shown that epithets cannot have pronouns as their antecedents.[29]

2.3.4. Prosentential reference

Pronouns and words such as *such* and *so* may be PROSENTENTIALLY REFERENT. For example, consider (2-40) (due to Klappholz and Lockman 1975):

---

the hummingbird. The latter creature is but an inch overall. [From: Hepworth, John. Outsight: Shock! Horror! Giant bee stuffs Boeing 747. *Nation review*, 8(32), 25-31 May 1978, page 20.]

The intention in (iii) is clearly that *the latter creature* is to refer to *the Xylocopid*, not *the hummingbird*. These texts are not acceptable in my dialect, though some people do not seem to mind (i) at least. For more of this, and its implications for transformational grammar, see Postal (1976).

[28]John and Mary are those playful characters well-loved by all readers of Schank (1975 and others).

[29]Apparent counterexamples to this can be explained as cataphora. For example, (i) parallels the structure of (ii) rather than (iii):

(i) When he entered the store, the poor bastard was robbed.
(ii) When he entered the store, Daryel was robbed.
(iii) When Daryel entered the store, he was robbed.

(2-40) The president was shot while riding in a motorcade down a major Dallas boulevard today; <u>it</u> caused a panic on Wall Street.[30]

Here, *it* does not refer to any of the preceding noun phrases, but to the whole situation of the president being shot while riding in a motorcade down a major Dallas boulevard today. In the next example (from Anderson 1976) *so* refers to a complete embedded sentence:

(2-41) Your wife was under the impression that you would be away tonight, and as you can see, I thought <u>so</u> too.

More than just a single sentence may be so referenced. For example, the first sentence of Chapter 11 of Tuchman's *A distant mirror* is (2-42):

(2-42) <u>Such</u> was the France to which Coucy returned in 1367.[31]

Such refers to the essence of all of Chapter 10.

2.3.5. Strained anaphora

Lakoff and Ross (1972) point out the frequent idiolectic acceptability of sentences like (2-43):

(2-43) John became a guitarist because he thought that <u>it</u> was a beautiful instrument.

The anaphor refers to the guitar, although this is only brought into consciousness by the noun phrase *guitarist*. Watt (1975) has called this phenomenon STRAINED ANAPHORA. Lakoff and Ross develop syntactic rules which explain why (2-43) is acceptable, but (2-44) and (2-45) are not:

(2-44) *The guitarist bought a new <u>one</u>.

(2-45) *John was a guitarist until he lost <u>it</u> on the subway.

In general, the antecedents of strained anaphors must be lexically similar to the actual words used in the text, such as *guitar* being similar to *guitarist*. Thus informants generally find (2-46) less acceptable than (2-43):

---

[30]Some instances of this type of sentence are idiolectically unacceptable to some people.

[31]Tuchman, Barbara Wertheim. *A distant mirror: The calamitous 14th century*. New York: Knopf, 21 September 1978, page 232.

(2-46) ?John became a flautist because he thought that it was a beautiful instrument.

Sentence (2-47) (due to Watt (1975:111)) is an apparent counterexample, in which the anaphor is not morphologically similar to its antecedent at all:

(2-47) The government's decision to annex Baja California as the fifty-fourth state was the second blow to freedom in as many weeks.

However, the lexical relationship seems to be enough for the anaphor to work like that of (2-43) (see also Watt 1973, 1975).

All this does not mean that such anaphors refer to the surface structure (or something just under the skin), and ignore semantics; for if this were the case, we could use the fact that *a ruler* can mean both a sovereign and a measuring stick to rewrite (2-48) as (2-49) (due to Carlson and Martin 1975):[32]

(2-48) The king picked up a measuring instrument and measured the lamp.

(2-49) *The ruler picked one up and measured the lamp.

Exactly what role semantics plays in this phenomenon is not clear. As Watt (1973) points out, the mere fact that *father* means *one who has sired a child*

---

[32]There are punning exceptions to this — a sort of non-elliptic syllepsis — varying in acceptability. Carlson and Martin (1975) offer (i) and (ii); the first is generally accepted, the second not:

(i) Henry Block even looks like one.[33]

(ii) *Frank Church has never been in one.

My explanation for the difference in acceptability is that the name must be sufficiently unusual for the hearer to notice its double meaning even before the punning anaphor is encountered in the text. Hence, we have:

(iii)*Norman Smith is descended from one. [From which: a Norman or a smith?]

(iv)*Kim Spencer wears one.

(v) Nadia Talent is full of it.

(vi)Tom Collins drinks lots of them.

Such puns really do turn up in real world text, as (vii) [from: *Time*, *109*(22), 30 May 1977] shows:

(vii)Not all the aliens are bad however. One who is not is Chewbacca (he doesn't), the 8-ft.-tall wookie.

True (elliptic) syllepsis, as for example in (viii) (after Webber (1978a:105), who labels it zeugma),[34] involves a similar kind of resolution:

(viii)Ross takes sugar in his coffee, ∮ pride in his appearance, and ∮ offence at the slightest innuendo.

Non-elliptic zeugma (that is, metaphor combined with syllepsis) probably don't exist in coherent English; elliptic zeugma is bad enough.

[33]It is also possible to interpret this text as meaning *Henry Block even looks like a Henry Block*, where a name like Henry Block is supposed to have associated with it a stereotyped image that a person with that name allegedly resembles:

(i) I just met someone named Archie Bunker, and, by jove, he even looks like one.

[34]Authorities disagree on where syllepsis and zeugma differ from one another. I follow here the terminology of Fowler's *Modern English usage* (1968).

2.3.5 Strained anaphora

does not permit (2-51) (after Watt 1973:461) to be derived from (2-50):

(2-50) Ross has sired a child, but none of his friends have seen it.

(2-51) *Ross is a father, but none of his friends have seen it.

That is, *father* is an ANAPHORIC ISLAND (Postal 1969) in (2-50). Yet in the same paper, Watt offers this alarming example (1973:486):

(2-52) Ross is already a father THREE TIMES OVER, but Clive hasn't even had ONE ϕ yet.

A fortiori:

(2-53) Ross is already a father THREE TIMES OVER, but Sue hasn't even had ONE ϕ yet.

That is, adding contrastive stress can turn an anaphoric island into a penetrable reef. (See section 7.1 for a possible explanation for this).

2.3.6. Difficult indefinite uses of *one*

A phenomenon which at first seems to be related to strained anaphora is the indefinite *one*, as in this text:

(2-54) Smoking gives one cancer.

This could be rephrased thus:

(2-55) Smoking gives {a | the} {smoker | person who smokes} cancer.

This seems to parallel the case of (2-43) above. However, things are not so simple. Consider:

(2-56) My boss makes one work hard.

(2-57) Malcolm Fraser makes one sick.

(2-58) Plutonium in the atmosphere makes one sick.

These mean, respectively:

(2-59) My boss makes all those people he supervises work hard.

(2-60) Malcolm Fraser makes everyone who is aware of him sick.

(2-61) Plutonium in the atmosphere makes everyone sick.

In each case, *one* means *all those whom <the subject of the sentence> affects* —
again, an item implicitly placed in consciousness. This also holds for (2-54).
Thus, we see that indefinite *one* is not a particular case of strained anaphora.

> *Have you seen my wife, Mr Jones?*
> *Do you know what it's like on the outside?*
> — *Robin and Barry Gibb* [35]

2.3.7. Non-referential pronouns

Some instances of the pronoun *it* don't refer to anything, and hence are not
anaphors, and some have referents defined by convention which need not be
present in consciousness. It is necessary to recognize all these when they are
found, lest precious hours be lost in bootless searches for textual referents.

Consider (2-62):

(2-62) It is fortunate that Nadia will never read this thesis.

This is a simple case of a dummy subject in a cleft sentence, derived from (2-
63), and the *it* is essentially meaningless: [36]

(2-63) That Nadia will never read this thesis is fortunate.

Note that syntax alone is not enough to identify the dummy *it*. In (2-64) *it* is a
dummy subject, but in (2-65) it could refer to *the cat*.

(2-64) This thesis contains many facts that would embarrass Nadia if she
knew they were being published. It is therefore fortunate that
Nadia will never read this thesis.

(2-65) If Nadia were to read this thesis, she would probably get so mad that
she would kick the cat. It is therefore fortunate that Nadia will
never read this thesis.

However, cleft interpretation seems to be the default in (2-65).

Some pronouns have conventional unspecified referents, as in this:

---

[35] From: New York mining disaster, 1941. On: Bee Gees. *Best of Bee Gees*. LP recording, Poly-
dor 5837063.

[36] One could say, for convenience, that it does have a referent, namely *that Nadia will never
read this thesis*, but this is merely playing with the definition of *referent*. There is, notwithstanding this, a clear qualitiative difference between this and other uses of the word *it*.

(2-66) It is half past two.

This could be restated thus:

(2-67) The time is half past two.

But the same process cannot, of course, be applied to (2-68) to give (2-69):

(2-68) It is half a lamington.

(2-69) *The time is half a lamington.[37]

In general, we have to be on the lookout for cases where *it* means by convention *the time*. Care is required, as we see here:

(2-70) How late is it? − It's ten to one.

(2-71) What's the starting price of Pervert's Delight? − It's ten to one.

There are other awkward cases, too.[38]

---

[37] This sentence is unacceptable for selectional or semantic reasons, while it is syntax that prevents (i) from being optionally rendered as (ii):

(i) What time is it.

(ii) *What time is the time?

[38] The question of these uses of *it* is complex and the only important point here is that they must be recognized by an anaphor resolver to avoid wasting time on fruitless searches for their referents.

Some of the problems in this area can be seen by considering (i):

(i) It is raining.

Unlike the case of *the time*, we cannot simply eliminate this sentence's *it* by rephrasing:

(ii) *{The sky | The weather} is raining.

But note also that (iii) is an acceptable sentence, although (iv) is strange to most people:

(iii)It was half past two and raining when Sue finally arrived.

(iv)?It was raining and half past two when Sue finally arrived.

Sentence (iii) suggests that *it* can mean both the time and the weather taken together − perhaps the general state of affairs. The strangeness of (iv) then needs to be explained. I leave this as an exercise for the reader.

The question of how and why *it* actually appears in these sentences is a matter of much debate in linguistics. Sentences like (v) (due to Morgan 1968) are even harder than (i) to rephrase without it:

(v) It is dark outside.

However, such sentences may have non-dummy subjects in other languages, indicating the presence of a subject in a deep, language-independent representation of the sentence. For example, in German, the dummy-subject sentence (vi) translates into English as (vii) with a substantial subject:

(vi)Es klingelt. [Literally, "It rings".]

(vii)Someone is ringing.

See Morgan (1968) for a slightly different approach to this question.

2.3.7 Non-referential pronouns

2.3.8. Pro-verbs

The only English pro-verbs are forms of *to do* as in (2-72) and (2-73):

(2-72) Daryel thinks like I do.

(2-73) When Ross orders sweet and sour fried short soup, Nadia does too.

The antecedents are, respectively, the VPs[39] *thinks* and *orders sweet and sour fried short soup*.

Under certain conditions the antecedent can be two or more VPs. Nash-Webber and Sag (1978) cite this example:

(2-74) She walks and she chews gum. Jerry does too, but not at the same time.

Of course, not all occurrences of *to do* are anaphoric: it can also mean *to perform <some task>*, and it can be a meaningless auxiliary:

(2-75) Nadia did her exercises.

(2-76) Ross does not like lychees with ice cream.

2.3.9. Proactions

When used in conjunction with *so, it* or demonstratives, *do* can reference ACTIONS in a manner which is almost prosentential. Consider:

(2-77) Daryel frequently goes to the cupboard, where he secretly pours himself a glass of Cointreau. He drinks it in one gulp. Sue does it too, but less discreetly.

---

[39]Halliday and Hasan (1976:114-115) give examples in which *do* replaces only part of a verb phrase:

  (i) Does Granny look after you every day? − She can't do at weekends, as she has to go to her own house.

  (ii) Mrs Birling: I don't understand you, Inspector.
     Inspector: You mean you don't choose to do, Mrs Birling. [From: Priestly, J B. *An inspector calls*. in: *The plays of J B Priestly*, Heinemann, volume 3.]

  (iii)What are you doing here? − We're mycologists, and we're looking for edible mushrooms. − Yes, we are doing too.

However, this usage is acceptable only in a British dialect of English; informants who were speakers of Canadian, American or Australian English immediately marked such sentences as British, and said that their dialect would not generate them. These dialects would use an ellipsis instead of *do*.

(2-78) Ross makes his dinner on weekdays, but when she stays the week-end Sue <u>does it</u> for him.

(2-79) Nadia removed a herring from her pocket and began to fillet it. Ross <u>did so</u> too.

In each of these texts, the PROACTIONAL anaphor refers not to the previous events but to the action therein: to the act of taking a herring from a pocket and beginning to fillet it, rather than Nadia's specific performance of that act. Note in particular that (2-79) does not mean that Ross removed the herring from Nadia's pocket, but rather from his own, and in (2-77), Sue pours herself, not Daryel, a glass of Cointreau. However in (2-78) Sue cooks Ross's dinner, not her own.

There is no firm dividing line between proactions and pro-verbs: (2-73) could have *does it* or *does so* in place of *does* without changing its meaning.

2.3.10. Proadjectives

Postal (1969:205) points out that words like *such* are anaphoric in texts like these:

(2-80) I was looking for a purple wombat, but I couldn't find <u>such</u> a wombat.

(2-81) I was looking for a wombat which spoke English, but I couldn't find <u>such</u> a wombat.

Such references are PROADJECTIVAL, or, in Postal's term, PRORELATIVE, referring here to *purple* [*wombat*] and [*wombat*] *which spoke English*. Often the antecedent is only implicit, as in (2-82):

(2-82) Ross came rocketing out the door and tripped over Nadia's nar-balek, which bounced off and cowered under the garage. <u>Such</u> situations have been a common occurrence since the vacation started.

Here, the antecedent for *such* [*situations*] is not [*situations*] *in which Ross comes rocketing* . . . but rather something like *chaotic* [*situations*]. See also Halliday and Hasan (1976:76-87).[40]

---

[40] In bureaucratese and legalese, *said* can be used as a proadjective for very explicit discourse cohesion:

(i) I bequeath absolutely my bandicoot Herbert to Ross Frederick Andrews of 79 Lowanna Street Braddon in the Australian Capital Territory provided that the <u>said</u> Ross Frederick Andrews shall keep feed and generally maintain the <u>said</u> bandicoot in good health order and condition.

The said Ross Frederick Andrews means *Ross Frederick Andrews of 79 Lowanna Street Braddon in the Australian Capital Territory*. The *saids* serve to explicitly prevent the condition be-

2.3.11. Temporal references

The word *then* can be used as a anaphoric reference to a time or an event, as can *at that time*:

(2-83) In the mid-sixties, free love was rampant across campus. It was <u>then</u> that Sue turned to Scientology.

(2-84) In the mid-sixties, free love was rampant across campus. <u>At that time</u>, however, bisexuality had not come into vogue.

Many temporal relations such as *afterwards* are anaphoric, in the sense that the time they are relating to is also a referent determined like that of an anaphor. In (2-85), *many years later* implies a reference to *the mid-sixties*, in a very similar manner (though of course with different meaning) to the *then* of (2-83):

(2-85) In the mid-sixties, free love was rampant across campus. <u>Many years later</u> Sue turned to Scientology.

2.3.12. Locative references

The word *there* is often an anaphoric reference to a place:

(2-86) The Church of Scientology met in a secret room behind the local Colonel Sanders' chicken stand. Sue had her first dianetic experience <u>there</u>.

Locative relations, like temporal relations, may also reference anaphorically:

(2-87) The Church of Scientology met in a secret room behind the local Colonel Sanders' chicken stand. <u>Across the street</u> was a McDonald's where the Bokononists and The Church Of God The Utterly Indifferent had their meetings.

---

ing satisfied by a different Ross Frederick Andrews, or by the maintenance of a different bandicoot.

2.3.13. Ellipsis: The ultimate anaphor!

Some anaphors are completely null. In (2-88):

(2-88) Ross took Nadia and Sue ϕ Daryel.

the word *took* has been elided. A whole VP may be elided:

(2-89) Nadia brought the food for the picnic, and Daryel ϕ the wine.

Here the elided VP is *brought to the picnic*. VP ellipsis cannot in general be exophoric (see Hankamer 1978; cf Schachter 1977 and Hankamer and Sag 1976).

The above examples illustrated VP ellipsis. However almost any part of a sentence can be elided:

(2-90) Ross carefully folded his trousers and ϕ climbed into bed.

(2-91) Who put this bewildered baby bandicoot in Barbara's biscuit barrel?
      − Ross ϕ.

In (2-90), the subject NP *Ross* is elided, and in (2-91) only the subject NP remains after the removal of *put that bewildered baby bandicoot in Barbara's biscuit barrel*. This latter kind of ellipsis is very common in answers to questions, so it is important that it be understood by any system which accepts natural language answers to queries.[41]

2.3.14. An awkward miscellany

The following examples are awkward exceptions to normal pronominalization:

(2-92) Andy sends the *1978 World Book Science Year Annual* to Lorri Dunn, 12, of Visalia, Calif., for her question:

---

[41]It should be noted that not all "syntactic gaps" are anaphoric. Thomas (1979) distinguishes ELISION and NON-REALIZATION, which are non-anaphoric, from true ellipsis, which requires context for its resolution. Elision is the removal of certain words, usually in informal speech, that may be recovered by applying certain conventional rules of conversation which Thomas details. An example:

(i) ϕ Got the tickets?

Non-realization is the syntactic removal, at a level below the surface, of elements that do not require recovery at all. An example of this is the non-appearance of [by] *someone* when (ii) is passivized to become (iii):

(ii) Someone murdered Jones.

(iii) Jones was murdered.

Why is <u>it</u> called a gunny sack?[42]

(2-93) Nadia: Is <u>it</u> pronounced ''tom-AY-to'' or ''tom-AH-to''?
Ross: Is WHAT pronounced ''tom-AY-to'' or ''tom-AH-to''?[43]

One could dismiss (2-92) as an illiteracy − it is unacceptable in my idiolect − but (2-93) is quite acceptable.[44] Another version of (2-92) is also mysterious:

(2-94) Why is a gunny sack <u>so-called</u>?

Here so-called is an adjective which refers to a noun phrase − a most unusual state of affairs. It may be objected that the referent here is the adjective gunny, not the NP gunny sack. But consider:

(2-95) Why is psittacosis <u>so-called</u>?
(2-96) Why is rappelling <u>so-called</u>?

Here the referents are unquestionably NPs. Note that in (2-96) the NP is a gerund; this seems to be the only way to ask such a question about a verb.

---

[42]From: Andy. Ask Andy. The province, 11 July 1978, page 14.

[43]Old joke, recently resurrected on the television series The muppet show.

[44]That Nadia's question in (2-93) is well-formed is shown by Ross's reply being humorous. The humour relies on Nadia's question being quite acceptable, although based on a prototype that normally wouldn't be. See Hirst (1979) for more discussion.

2.3.15. Summary of anaphors

The following table summarizes the different types of anaphor we have seen:

Type of anaphor	Lexical Realization
Pronominal	
• pronouns	*he, she, it, they, one,* . . .
• epithets	*the idiot, that stinking lump of camel excrement,* . . .
• surface count	*the former, the latter, same,* low ordinals, . . .
Prosentential	*it, so,* . . .
Pro-verbial	*do*
Proactional	*do so, do it*
Proadjectival/prorelative	*such, so,* . . .
Temporal	*then,* temporal relations
Locative	*there,* locative relations
Ellipsis	ϕ

2.4. Where does anaphora end?

The previous section dealt with various anaphoric proforms. The spirit of anaphora is not limited to proforms, however. This section examines some other linguistic constructions that can be used in an anaphor-like manner.

2.4.1. Paraphrase

Paraphrase is a restatement of a part of a text in different words to clarify the intended meaning or for stylistic reasons. When a noun phrase is subsequently paraphrased in a text, the result is often anaphor-like. Indeed, it is not clear where anaphora ends and paraphrase begins. Consider these examples:

(2-97) The man carrying the aeolian harp stumbled and for a moment Sue thought <u>the man</u> would fall.

(2-98) Sue watched the man from her hiding place. <u>The man</u> had an aeolian harp, which he was holding above his head in an attempt to make it play.

(2-99) At first Ross couldn't locate the Pope. Then he looked up, and saw <u>the beloved pontiff</u> floating gently to earth.

In (2-97), *the man* (second occurrence) refers to the man carrying the aeolian harp. Such INCOMPLETE REPETITIONS clearly fit our definition of an anaphor, although people may not always classify them as such. The problem of understanding them differs from the case where a proform is used only in the quantity of information given in the reference. Programs such as Bobrow's (1964) STUDENT (see section 3.1.1) have dealt with such incompletes, using heuristics to equate them with their referent. Further, as in (2-98), a single complete repetition is again anaphor-like in the way it performs a subsequent reference to the man with the aeolian harp.

In (2-99), *the beloved pontiff* refers to the Pope. Although this is not an abbreviation,[45] but rather a disabbreviation, it again shares the spirit of anaphora, and again the problem of understanding and making the connection is similar.[46]

The style of writing in which the paraphrases are not just lexically longer but are used to give more information than the original noun phrase occurs frequently in North American newspaper reports; (2-100) demonstrates this style:

(2-100)   BIG BEN FATIGUED

LONDON — With a rattle and a bang, London's famous landmark, the Big Ben clock, ground to a halt today at 4:46 a.m.

<u>The 117-year-old timepiece</u> apparently was the victim of metal fatigue.[47]

Here the paraphrase (underlined) gives us new information, in this case about the age of the clock. We can make the connection easily since *the . . . timepiece* clearly points back to *the . . . clock*. (If the noun phrase had been *a . . . timepiece*, then the indefinite article would mean that a different clock was being talked about.)

In the next example, there is no definite article or other pointer to help resolve the coreference:

---

[45] It is not an epithet either, as it can be stressed if spoken.

[46] Could we take this analysis backwards, and construe *the Pope* as a cataphor of *the beloved pontiff* as we did in footnote 29? We probably cannot since, without more context, we could replace the latter but not the former with the anaphor *him*. In other words, in the absence of a compelling reason to do so we are loathe to allow the possibility of a cataphoric noun phrase existing where a cataphoric pronoun could not.

[47] Associated Press, 5 August 1976.

(2-101) CHOWCHILLA, Calif. — Two men charged with the abduction of 26 school children appeared in a packed courtroom today amid tight security and pleaded not guilty to 43 charges of kidnap and robbery. James Schoenfeld and Frederick Woods both 24, appeared in justice court with Schoenfeld's brother, Richard, 22, who entered a plea of not guilty to the same charges a week ago.[48]

The two paragraphs of (2-101) could be two separate court report summaries; only our knowledge of the style (and perhaps previous knowledge of the Chowchilla kidnapping case) allows us to detect that *James Schoenfeld and Frederick Woods* are the *two men* of the previous paragraph, and *justice court* is *a packed courtroom*.

It is necessary, however, that the identity of the paraphrase and its referent be reasonably easy to infer. Informants frequently failed to recognize the paraphrase in this text:

(2-102) Most of the city's federal buildings were dark, but chandeliers shone brightly from the National Portrait Gallery. Inside the building in which Walt Whitman once read his poetry to wounded Union troops and Abe Lincoln held his second Inaugural Ball, a black-tie assemblage of guests stood chatting.[49]

In fact, *the building in which Walt Whitman once read his poetry to wounded Union troops and Abe Lincoln held his second Inaugural Ball* is the previously-mentioned National Portrait Gallery, but many readers assume two separate buildings are being spoken of, apparently due to the difficulty of detecting the paraphrase in such convoluted prose.

Not only NPs but also sentences and situations may be paraphrased. In this example (after Phillips 1975) *the mistake* refers prosententially to the whole preceding sentence:

(2-103) Ross put his car into reverse instead of drive and hit a wall. The mistake cost him two hundred dollars.

2.4.2. Definite reference

The anaphora and paraphrase problems are actually special cases of the definite reference problem. This is illustrated in the next two examples:

---

[48] Associated Press, 4 August 1976.

[49] From: Davidson, Ralph P. A letter from the publisher. *Time, 111*(20), 15 May 1978.

(2-104) Nadia bought a DECsystem-10. <u>The processor</u> is a KL10B.

The scene for the second example is similar to that for (2-20), except that this time the guest is admiring the host's new car. The host comes up and remarks:

(2-105) Because I'm a nostalgic horse racing fan, I've had <u>the speedometer</u> marked in furlongs per hour.

In these examples, the NPs *the processor* and *the speedometer* mean those of the DECsystem-10 and the car,[50] respectively, and semantically stand in the relation PART OF to those antecedents. Other possible relations include SUBSET OF (Klappholz and Lockman 1975), and ASPECT or ATTRIBUTE OF.[51] We see that anaphora and paraphrase are merely cases of coreferentiality where the relation is IS IDENTICAL TO.

Sometimes a coreference relationship is not one of those just mentioned, but rather is one determined by inference (Clark 1975). Consider this example:

(2-106) "It's nice having dinner with candles, but there's something funny about the two we've got tonight", Carol said. "They were the same length when you first lit them. Look at them now."

John chuckled. "<u>The girl</u> did say one would burn for four hours and the other for five", he replied. "Now one is twice as long as the other."

They had been burning for the same time, of course. How long was that?[52]

The relationship between *the candle* and *the girl* is that the latter presumably is the salesperson who sold John the former. To determine this requires a high level of inference, such as that performed in the MARGIE system (Schank, Goldman, Rieger and Riesbeck 1975; Rieger 1975), and we would not want to say that there is an intrinsic semantic relation between girls and candles. A simplistic resolution algorithm would probably have decided that *the girl* in this example

---

[50]We regard *the speedometer* as a reference to *the car* with the latter as antecedent, rather than a direct reference to *the speedometer* as an item in consciousness, on the reasonable assumption that the speedometer itself was not in the listener's consciousness. Clearly, the speaker could have referenced ANY part of the car from the engine through to the little switch that makes the light come on when you open the door but it is unlikely that the listener would have had all these parts in consciousness.

[51]Examples of these relations:
SUBSET OF:

(i) The Department has graduated five students this year. <u>The PhDs</u> were all in AI.

ASPECT or ATTRIBUTE OF:

(ii) For Christmas that year, Julian gave Sissy a miniature Tyrolean village. <u>The craftsmanship</u> was remarkable. [From: Robbins, Tom. *Even cowgirls get the blues*. New York: Bantam, 1977, page 191.]

Klappholz and Lockman (1975) suggest MEMBER OF as another possible relation, but I am not convinced that it differs in practice from PART OF.

[52]From: Hunter, J A H. Figure it out. *The Canberra times*, 26 October 1977, page 25.

2.4.2 Definite reference

was *Carol.*

Between the extremes of a fixed relation like ASPECT OF and inferred relation like that in (2-106) is the vague relation CLOSELY ASSOCIATED WITH:

(2-107) The manager ushered Sue and Nadia into his <u>office</u> with obvious embarrassment.

The concept of *office* is closely associated with the concept of *manager*, through some fairly direct piece of world knowledge like (WORKS-IN MANAGER OFFICE). In section 5.2.2 we will see how this sort of relation might be handled.

2.5. Types of reference

Having reviewed the different sorts of anaphora in English, we are now in a position to make another elaboration of our definition of anaphora. We will distinguish between IDENTITY OF SENSE ANAPHORA[53] (ISA) and IDENTITY OF REFERENCE ANAPHORA (IRA).[54]

An IRA is an anaphor which denotes the same entity as its antecedent. For example, in (2-108)

(2-108) Ross made a gherkin sandwich and ate <u>it</u>.

it refers to the very same gherkin sandwich that Ross made. An ISA denotes not the same entity as its antecedent, but one of a similar description. Wasow (1975) offers this example:

(2-109) The man who gave his paycheck to his wife was wiser than the man who gave <u>it</u> to his mistress.

Clearly, *it* means the second man's paycheck, not the first man's.

Since the meaning of a text may depend on whether an anaphor is an ISA or an IRA, it is necessary for the complete computer NLU system to be able to tell them apart. This requires the use of semantics and world knowledge. In (2-109), we know *it* is an ISA because, we assume, each man has a paycheck, and an item cannot be given independently to two people at once.

Occasionally below, we will follow Partee (1978) in distinguishing between anaphors which function as bound variables and other anaphors. For example, in (2-110):

---

[53]The term is due to Grinder and Postal (1971), who abbreviate it "I - S = A" ['sic].

[54]An alternative terminology (Nash-Webber 1976): ISA are like DESCRIPTIONAL anaphora, and IRA like DENOTATIONAL anaphora.

(2-110) No child will admit that <u>he</u> is sleepy.

he is a bound variable anaphor which functions as a place-holder for *child*, much as the bound variable *x* does in the logical form (2-111):

(2-111) $\neg(\exists x:\text{child})$. will-admit-sleepiness x

2.6. Ambiguity in anaphora and default antecedents

Many anaphors, like that of (2-112):

(2-112) Ross told Daryel <u>he</u> had passed the exam.

are ambiguous — *he* could be either Ross or Daryel. However, some which are theoretically ambiguous are in practice not:

(2-113) Daryel told Ross <u>he</u>[(1)] was the ugliest person <u>he</u>[(2)] knew of.

In this example, each occurrence of *he* could mean either Daryel or Ross, giving a total of four readings for the sentence. Yet most people immediately assume that *he*[(1)] is Ross and *he*[(2)] is Daryel without even noticing some or all of the other readings.

   This indicates that in many cases of ambiguous anaphors there is a PRE-FERRED or DEFAULT ANTECEDENT, which is taken as the correct one in the absence of contraindicating context or knowledge. The qualification is necessary, as a sentence like (2-113) can be disambiguated by context:

(2-114) Daryel examined his face disapprovingly in the mirror. When Ross asked him what conclusions he came to, Daryel told Ross <u>he</u> was the ugliest person <u>he</u> knew of.

Both *he*s refer to Daryel here.

   More examples to convince the doubtful:

(2-115) BRISBANE — A terrific right rip from Hector Thompson dropped Ross Eadie at Sandgate on Friday night and won <u>him</u> the Australian welterweight boxing title.[55]

No informant to whom I showed this saw any ambiguity. They were clearly using their knowledge of boxing to infer, without realising it, that it was Thompson (and not Eadie) who won the boxing title. To see that world knowledge is

---

[55]From: *The Canberra times*, 25 May 1977.

the key factor here, we need only consider this report on the sport of dropping, the object of which is to be the first one dropped:

(2-116)   BRISBANE — A terrific right rip from Hector Thompson dropped Ross Eadie at Sandgate on Friday night and won <u>him</u> the Australian welterweight dropping title.

Not all ambiguous anaphors have a default; this one probably doesn't:

(2-117)   SALEM, Ore. — Police Chief Paul Arritola of nearby Jordan Valley runs what could be the most profitable radar speed trap on the continent.

Documents filed here in connection with suit against him show that he collected $102,117 in traffic fines last year. Under his contract with this community of 210 people, he gets all the revenue, less the state's share and the cost of running his two-man department. In 1978, <u>that</u> worked out to $70,000.

Said Jordan Valley Mayor Ed Krupp: "I'd rather have no comment."[56]

There was no consensus among informants as to whether the police chief ended up with $70,000 or $32,000 because of the ambiguity of *that*. The former case was however slightly preferred (and was probably intended by the writer), since the overall theme of the text is the amount of money that the police chief collected.

That there can, however, be a default referent which is neither the subject nor the theme (see also section 4.1) is shown by this example:

(2-118)   The FBI's role is to ensure our country's freedom and be ever watchful of those who threaten <u>it</u>.[57]

Most informants took *it* to be *our country's freedom* or *our country* (these referents having more or less the same meaning in this context, I assume), rather than *the FBI* or *the FBI's role*, which are also semantically plausible referents, and which are, respectively, the theme and the subject. (Of course, there are those who say that all four candidates have more or less the same meaning in this context.)

Defaults will be discussed further in section 6.5.

An anaphor which can be read as both an IRA and an ISA can make a text ambiguous:

(2-119)   Ross likes his hair short, but Daryel likes <u>it</u> long.

It can be Ross's hair, if an IRA, or Daryel's, if an ISA.

---

[56]From: *The Vancouver express*, 9 March 1979, page A5.

[57]Slightly modified from: Sherman, Craig. [Letter]. *Time*, *111*(20), 15 May 1978.

2.6 Ambiguity in anaphora and default antecedents

Ambiguity may arise only after another anaphor is resolved. The text (2-120) (after Grinder and Postal 1971):

(2-120) Ross loves his wife and Daryel <u>does</u> too.

is ambiguous as to whose wife Daryel loves — his own or Ross's; that is, when *does* is macro-expanded (Hirst 1976b) as *loves his wife*, the *his* is ambiguous.[58] This phenomenon is called SLOPPY IDENTITY.[59]

Sometimes, ambiguities can be resolved by simple lexical information. For example, (2-121) is NOT ambiguous in the same way that (2-120) is, simply because it is inherent in nose twitching that one can only do it to one's own nose:

(2-121) Nadia was able to twitch her nose and Ross was ϕ too.[60]

Similarly, (2-122) is only two ways ambiguous and not four ways as is (2-112), since both anaphors must be coreferential:

(2-122) Ross told Daryel <u>he</u> was able to twitch <u>his</u> nose.

Verb symmetry and reflexivity can also inhibit ambiguity. For example, for all entities A and B *A looks like B* implies *B looks like A*, and *A looks like A* is identically true for all A. Hence (2-123), superficially four ways ambiguous, can only have one meaning, since the two readings with the anaphors coreferential can be dismissed as tautologies (which violate conversational postulates (Gordon and Lakoff 1971; Grice 1975)) and the other two readings are semantically identical:

(2-123) People like dogs because <u>they</u> look like <u>them</u>.

We would not want an NLU system to waste time (or infinitely loop) trying to decide if "people look like dogs" is better than "dogs look like people".

What does all this portend for a computer NLU system? Clearly, it sets certain minimum requirements. A system will need:

 1 knowledge about words and their uses;

 2 world knowledge;

---

[58]The sentence is unambiguous if we happen to know that Daryel is not married.

[59]Related to the sloppy identity problem is the problem of MISSING ANTECEDENTS, described by Grinder and Postal (1971) who provide this example:

(i) My uncle doesn't have a spouse, but your aunt does and <u>he</u> is lying on the floor.

The referent of *he* is clearly *your aunt's spouse*. This can only be resolved after the ISA proverb *does* is properly interpreted or macro-expanded as *has a spouse*.

[60]Even if Ross had the power to make Nadia's nose twitch, by Pavlovian conditioning for example, we could not express this fact with (2-121), instead having to say something like (i):

(i) Nadia was able to make her nose twitch and Ross was ϕ too

2.6 Ambiguity in anaphora and default antecedents

2 a method of determining default antecedents; and

4 inference mechanisms to apply to 1–3 above and to the meaning of the discourse itself.

2.7. Summary and discussion

In this chapter, I have tried to do these things:

1 define with reasonable precision what anaphora and reference are;

2 give examples of various types of anaphora;

3 demonstrate that a referent can be almost anything in the listener's consciousness, be it explicit or implicit in the discourse, or not in the discourse at all; and

4 show how and why anaphora and reference can be a problem for NLU by computer, and how they are interrelated with other problems in NLU;

5 show that anaphor resolution requires world knowledge, word meaning, inference and default referents.

This chapter, then, has been essentially the statement of a problem. The rest of this thesis looks at solutions to the problem. Because of the fuzziness of the boundary between anaphora and paraphrase and other forms of reference, the problem has, unfortunately, a very fuzzy boundary. It follows by definition that any general resolver of definite reference (clearly a desirable AI goal) will contain an anaphor resolver as a subset. It does not follow, however, that any anaphor resolver can be expanded into a definite reference resolver. Perhaps what is needed is not a happily independent anaphor resolver, but a more general solution to the problem of reference. However, such a solution may not exist, and even if it does, it may not be accessible to us in the near future. Therefore, an independent anaphor resolver is a good step to take next. In subsequent chapters, we shall sometimes, where it is fairly easy to do so, be general and address the problem of reference. At other times, we shall concentrate more particularly on anaphora. This is what AI workers call the vacillation paradigm.

Chapter 3

TRADITIONAL APPROACHES TO ANAPHORA

> *They went about and sang of Rāma's deeds; and Rāma*
> *heard of it, and he called an assembly of the Brāhmans*
> *and all kinds of grammarians . . . and the hermit chil-*
> *dren sang before them all.*
>   — *The Rāmāyana*[1]

In this chapter and Chapter 5 I describe and evaluate some of the approaches that have been taken to anaphora, with respect to NLU systems, over the past years. I have divided them very roughly into two classes: traditional and modern. The traditional systems tend not to recognize as a separate problem the question of what is or isn't in consciousness. Rather, they assume that, other things being equal, the set of possible referents is exactly the set of NPs (or whatever), from the whole of the preceding text, in strict order of recency. Their resolution methods tend to work at the sentence level, and may bring to bear world knowledge and low-level linguistic knowledge. Antecedents not explicit in the text are not handled. This characterization is of course a generalization; not all approaches classified as traditional fit this description in every detail. On the other hand, modern methods recognize the importance of focus and discourse-level knowledge for resolution. Implicit antecedents may also be handled.

In this chapter, I review the traditional methods; in Chapter 5, the modern methods are presented.

3.1. Some traditional systems

First we will look at some of the systems that employed traditional anaphor resolution methods.

---

[1]From the translation in: Coomaraswamy, Ananda K and The Sister Nivedita of Rāmakrishna–Vivekānanda (Margaret E Noble). *Myths of the Hindus & Buddhists*. [1] Harrap, 1913. [2] New York: Dover, 1967. page 110.

I lisp'd in Numbers.
— *Alexander Pope*[2]

3.1.1. STUDENT

The high-school algebra problem answering system STUDENT (Bobrow 1964), an early system with natural language input, has only a few limited heuristics for resolving anaphors and, more particularly, anaphor-like paraphrases and incomplete repetitions. For example, in a question such as (3-1):

(3-1) The number of soldiers the Russians have is half the number of guns they have. The number of guns is 7000. What is the number of soldiers they have?

the system will first try to solve the problem treating *the number of soldiers the Russians have* and *the number of soldiers they have* as two separate and distinct variables. Upon failure, it will eventually identify the two phrases by noting that they are identical up to the pronoun in the second. Similarly, it will identify *the number of guns* with *the number of guns they have* by the fact that the former is contained in and occurs after the latter. STUDENT does not actually resolve the pronouns at all. Phrases containing *this* are usually taken to refer to the consequence of the immediately preceding item without looking at the rest of the phrase. Thus, in (3-2):

(3-2) A number is multiplied by 6. This product is increased by 44.

the word *product* could be changed to *result* or *sasquatch* without changing the assumed referent of *this*. Cases like (3-3):

(3-3) The price of a radio is 69.70 dollars. This price is 15% less than the marked price.

are apparently resolved through the two occurrences of the word *price*.

Clearly, these simple heuristics are easily fooled since the sentence is not even parsed in any real sense. For example, in (3-4) the two references to sailors would not be matched up, although modifications to the heuristics may change this:

(3-4) The number of soldiers the Russians have is twice the number of sailors they have. The number of soldiers is 7000. How many sailors do the Russians have?

---

[2]From: An epistle to Dr Arbuthnot. 2 January 1735, line 128. in, inter alia: Pope, Alexander. *Imitations of Horace with an epistle to Dr Arbuthnot and the Epilogue to the Satires.* (= The Twickenham edition of the poems of Alexander Pope 4). London: Methuen, 1939.

However a sophisticated paraphrase of (3-4) would stand no chance:

(3-5) If the Russians have twice as many soldiers as sailors, and they have 7000 soldiers, how many sailors are there?

> *"No, no", said Anne. "That won't do. You must do something more than that."*
> *"But what? All the good jobs are taken, and all I can do is lisp in numbers."*
> *"Well, then, you must lisp", concluded Anne.*
> *— Aldous Leonard Huxley*[3]

3.1.2. SHRDLU

Winograd's (1971, 1972) celebrated SHRDLU system employs heuristics much more complex than those of STUDENT, providing impressive and, for the most part, sophisticated handling of anaphors, including references to earlier parts of the conversation between the program and its user. The most important aspect of SHRDLU's handling of anaphors is that in checking previous noun groups as possible referents, it does not seize the first likely candidate for use, but rather checks all possibilities in the preceding text and assigns each a rating whereby the most plausible answer is selected. If none clearly stands out as a winner, the user is asked for help in choosing between the serious contenders.

Gross heuristics cover some simpler cases. If *it* or *they* occurs twice in the same sentence, or in two adjacent sentences, the occurrences are assumed to be coreferential. This usually works, but there are, as always, easy counterexamples, such as (3-6) (from Minsky 1968):

(3-6) He put the box on the table. Because it wasn't level, it slid off.

An anaphor which is part of its own referent, as (3-7):

(3-7) a block which is bigger than anything which supports it

can be detected and interpreted correctly by SHRDLU without infinite regression. Reference to events, as in (3-8):

(3-8) Why did you do it?

is resolved through always remembering the last event referred to.

---

[3]From: *Crome yellow*. New York: Harper, 1922.

Some contrastive uses of *one* can be handled, as in (3-9):

(3-9) a big green pyramid and a little <u>one</u>

A list of pairs of words like *big* and *little* that are often used contrastively is employed to work out that *little one* here means *little green pyramid* and not *little pyramid* or *little big green pyramid*. This method assumes no redundant information is given. Suppose your universe had three pyramids: a big blue one, a big green one and a little blue one. Then the above interpretation of (3-9) would have you looking for a little green pyramid which you don't have, when the speaker obviously meant the little blue one. Although the *big* in (3-9) is redundant and has resulted in an erroneous interpretation, it is a perfectly acceptable phrase which reflects the way people often talk.

The methods used for *one* are also used for incompletes that are cardinal numbers, such as in (3-10):

(3-10) Find the red blocks and stack up <u>three</u>.

3.1.3. LSNLIS

The Lunar Sciences Natural Language Information System (LSNLIS — also known as LUNAR) (Woods, Kaplan and Nash-Webber 1972; Woods 1977) uses an ATN parser (Woods 1970) and a semantic interpreter based on the principles of pro-cedural semantics (Woods 1968).[4] It is in this latter component that the system resolves anaphoric references, giving full meaning to pronouns found in the parse tree.

The system distinguishes two classes of anaphors: PARTIAL and COMPLETE. A complete anaphor (of which there are three types) is a pronoun which refers to a complete antecedent noun phrase, while a partial one refers to only part of a preceding NP; that is, the first is an IRA and the second an ISA. (3-11) shows a complete anaphoric reference and (3-12) a partial one:

(3-11) Which coarse-grained rocks have been analyzed for cobalt? Which <u>ones</u> have been analyzed for strontium?

(3-12) Give me all analyses of sample 10046 for hydrogen. Give me <u>them</u> for oxygen.

Note that in (3-12), *them* refers to *all analyses of sample 10046*, whereas the NP in the antecedent sentence was *all analyses of sample 10046 for hydrogen*. Such partial anaphors are signalled by the presence of a relative clause or

---

[4]A useful overview of the whole LSNLIS system, together with a detailed critique of its anaphor handling capabilities, may be found in Nash-Webber (1976).

prepositional phrase modifying the pronoun; here it is *for oxygen*.

Partial anaphors are resolved by searching through antecedent noun phrases for one with a parallel syntactic and semantic structure. In (3-12), for example, the antecedent NP is found, and *for oxygen* substituted for *for hydrogen*. This method is not unlike Bobrow's in STUDENT (see section 3.1.1), but it works on the syntactic and semantic level rather than at the more superficial level of lexical matching with a little added syntax. It suffers however from the same basic limitation, namely that it can only resolve anaphors where the antecedent is of a similar structure. Neither (3-13) nor (3-14), for example, could have been used as the second sentence of (3-12):

(3-13) Give me the oxygen ones.

(3-14) Give me those that have been done for oxygen.

Three different methods are used for complete anaphoric references, the one chosen depending on the exact form of the anaphor. The first form includes a noun and uses the anaphor as a determiner:

(3-15) Do any breccias contain aluminium? What are those breccias?

The strategy used here is to search for a noun phrase whose head noun is *breccias*. Note that if the second sentence contained instead a paraphrase, such as *those samples*, this method would either find the wrong antecedent, or none at all, as there is no mechanism for recognizing the paraphrase.

The second form is a single pronoun:

(3-16) How much titanium is in type B rocks? How much silicon is in them?

In this case, more semantic information needs to be used. The semantic template which matches "ELEMENT BE IN" requires that the object of the verb be a SAMPLE, and this fact is used in searching for a suitable antecedent in this example. This is isomorphic to a weak use of a case-based approach (see sections 3.1.5 and 3.2.4).

The third type of complete anaphor is *one* and *ones*, as in (3-11). These are resolved either with or without modifiers like *too* and *also*. (Notice that if either of these modifiers were appended to (3-11), the meaning would be completely changed, the anaphor referring not to the first question but rather to its answer.) Resolution is by a method similar to that used for single pronouns.

The primary limitation of LSNLIS is that intrasentential anaphors cannot be resolved, because a noun phrase is not available as an antecedent until processing of the sentence containing it is complete.

3.1.4. MARGIE and SAM

So far, the natural language systems based on conceptual dependency theory (Schank 1973), MARGIE (Schank, Goldman, Rieger and Riesbeck 1975; Schank 1975) and SAM (Schank and the Yale AI Project 1975; Schank and Abelson 1977; Nelson 1978), have apparently not been able to handle any form of anaphor much beyond knowing that *he* always refers to John (a pathetic victim of social brutalization) and *she* to Mary (a pathetic victim of John, who frequently beats and murders her).

However, the Conceptual Memory section of MARGIE (Rieger 1975) is able to resolve some limited forms of definite reference by inference. Conceptual Memory operates upon nonlinguistic representations of concepts based on Schank's conceptual dependency theory, and can perform sixteen types of inference, including motivational, normative, causative and resultative. For example, if the system knows of two people named Andy, one an adult and one an infant, it can work out which is the subject of (3-17):

(3-17) Andy's diaper is wet.

That conceptual dependency—based systems should be so limited with respect to reference is disappointing, as conceptual dependency may prove to be an excellent framework for inference on anaphors (see section 3.2.6).

3.1.5. A case-driven parser

In his case-driven parser, Taylor (1975; Taylor and Rosenberg 1975) uses case analysis (Fillmore 1968, 1977) to resolve anaphors.

Pronouns are only encountered by the parser when a particular verb case is being sought, thereby giving much information about its referent. Previous sentences and nonsubordinate clauses[5] are searched for a referent that fits the case and which passes other tests, usually SHOULD-BE and MUST-BE predicates, to ensure that it fits semantically. As the search becomes more desperate, the SHOULD-BE tests are relaxed. Locative and dummy-subject anaphors can also be resolved.

The parser will always take the first candidate that passes all the tests as the referent. This occasionally leads to problems, where there are two or more acceptable candidates, but the first one found is not the correct one.

---

[5]Subordinate clauses in English can contain anaphors, but Taylor's system will not find them.

How is this done? By fucking around with syntax.
   — Tom Robbins[6]

3.1.6. Parse tree searching

An algorithm for searching a parse tree of a sentence to find the referent for a pronoun has been given by Jerry Hobbs (1976, 1977). The algorithm takes into consideration various syntactic constraints on pronominalization (see section 3.2.2) to search the tree in an optimal order such that the NP upon which it terminates is probably the antecedent of the pronoun at which the algorithm started. (For details of the algorithm, which is too long to give here, and an example of its use, see Hobbs (1976:8-13) or Hobbs (1977:2-7).)

Because the algorithm operates purely on the parse, it does not take into account the meaning of the text, nor can it find non-explicit antecedents. Nonetheless, Hobbs found that it gives the right answer a large proportion of the time.

To test the algorithm, Hobbs took text from an archaeology book, an Arthur Hailey novel and a copy of *Newsweek*. From each of these as much contiguous text as was necessary to obtain one hundred occurrences of pronouns was taken. He then applied the algorithm to each pronoun and counted the number of times it worked.[7] He reports (1976:25) that the algorithm worked 88 percent of the time, and 92 percent when augmented with simple selectional constraints. In many cases, the algorithm worked because there was only one available antecedent anyway; in the cases where there was more than one, the algorithm combined with selectional restrictions was correct for 82 percent of the time.

Clearly, the algorithm by itself is inadequate. However Hobbs suggests that it may still be useful, as it is computationally cheap compared to any semantic method of pronoun resolution. Because it is frequently necessary for semantic resolution methods to search for inference chains from reference to referent, time may frequently be saved, suggests Hobbs (1976:38), by using a bidirectional search starting at both the reference and the antecedent proposed by the algorithm, seeing if the two paths meet in the middle.

---

[6]From: *Even cowgirls get the blues*. New York: Bantam, 1977, page 379.

[7]To the best of my knowledge, Hobbs is the only worker in NLU to have ever quantitatively evaluated the efficacy of a language understanding mechanism on unrestricted real-world text in this manner. Clearly, such evaluation is frequently desirable.

3.1.7. Preference semantics

Wilks (1973b, 1975a, 1975b) describes an English to French translation system[8] which uses four levels of pronominal anaphor resolution depending on the type of anaphor and the mechanism needed to resolve it. The lowest level, type "A", uses only knowledge of individual lexeme meanings. For example, in (3-18):

> (3-18) Give the bananas to the monkeys although <u>they</u> are not ripe, because <u>they</u> are very hungry.

each *they* is interpreted correctly using the knowledge that monkeys, being animate, are likely to be hungry, and bananas, being a fruit, are likely to be (not) ripe. The system uses "fuzzy matching" to make such judgements; while it chooses the most likely match, future context or information may cause the decision to be reversed. The key to Wilks's system is very general rules which specify PREFERRED choices but don't require an irreversible commitment in case the present situation should turn out to be an exception to the rule.

If word meaning fails to find a unique referent for the pronoun, inference methods for type "B" anaphors — those that need analytic inference — or type "C" anaphors — those that require inference using real-world knowledge beyond simple word meanings — are brought in. These methods extract all case relationships from a template representation of the text and attempt to construct the shortest possible inference chain, not using real-world knowledge unless necessary.

If the anaphor is still unresolved after all this, "focus of attention" rules attempt to find the topic of the sentence to use as the referent.

Wilks's system of rules exhibiting undogmatic preferences, as well as his stratification of resolution requirements, is intuitively appealing, and appears the most promising of the approaches we have looked at; it could well be applied to forms of anaphora other than pronouns. My major disagreement is with Wilks's relegation of (rudimentary) discourse considerations to use only in last desperate attempts. I will show in the next chapter that they need to play a more important role.

3.1.8. Summary

We have seen six basic traditional approaches to anaphora and coreferentiality:

1. a few token heuristics;
2. more sophisticated heuristics with a semantic base;
3. a case-based grammar to give the heuristics extra power, using word meanings as well;

---

[8]For an unbiased description of Wilks's system, see Browse (1976).

4 lots and lots of undirected inference;

5 dumb parse-tree searching, with semantic operations to keep out of trouble;

6 a scheme of flexible preference semantics with word meanings and inference.

In the next section, we will evaluate in greater detail these and other approaches.

> *The Hodja was walking home when a man came up behind him and gave him a thump on the head. When the Hodja turned round, the man began to apologize, saying that he had taken him for a friend of his. The Hodja, however, was very angry at this assault upon his dignity, and dragged the man off to the court. It happened, however, that his assailant was a close friend of the cadi [magistrate], and after listening to the two parties in the dispute, the cadi said to his friend:*
>
> *"You are in the wrong. You shall pay the Hodja a farthing damages."*
>
> *His friend said that he had not that amount of money on him, and went off, saying he would get it.*
>
> *Hodja waited and waited, and still the man did not return. When an hour had passed, the Hodja got up and gave the cadi a mighty thump on the back of his head.*
>
> *"I can wait no longer", he said. "When he comes, the farthing is yours."[9]*

3.2. Abstraction of traditional approaches

Before continuing on to the discourse-oriented approaches to anaphora in the next two chapters, I would like to stand back and review the position so far.

It is a characteristic of research in NLU that, as in many new and smallish fields, the best way to describe an approach is to give the name of the person with whom it is generally associated. This is reflected in the organization of both section 3.1 and Chapter 5. However, in this section I would like to categorize approaches, divorcing them from people's names, and to formalize what we have seen so far.

---

[9]From: Charles Downing (reteller). *Tales of the Hodja*. Oxford University Press, 1964, page 10. This excerpt is recommended for anaphor resolvers not only as a useful moral lesson, but also as a good test of skill and ruggedness.

3.2.1. A formalization of the problem

David Klappholz and Abe Lockman (1975) (hereafter K&L), who were perhaps the first in NLU to even consider the problem of reference as a whole, sketch out the basics of a reference resolver. They see it as necessarily based upon and operating upon representations of meaning, a set of world knowledge and a memory of the FOCUS derived from each past sentence, including noun phrases, verb phrases, and events.[10] One then matches up anaphors with previous noun phrases and other constituents, and uses semantics to see what is a reasonable match and what isn't, hoping to avoid a combinatorial explosion with the aid of the world knowledge.

Specifically, K&L envisaged three focus sets — for noun-objects, events and time.[11] As each sentence comes in, a meaning representation is formed for it; then the focus sets are updated by adding entities from the new sentence, and discarding those from the nth previous sentence, which are now deemed too far back to be referred to. (K&L do not hazard any guess at what a good value for n is.) A hypothesis set of all triples (N_1, N_2, r) is generated, where N_1 is a reference needing resolution, N_2 is an entity in focus and r is a possible reference relation (see section 2.4.2). A judgement mechanism then tries to winnow the hypotheses with inference, semantics and knowledge, until a consistent set is left.

This method is, of course, what Winograd and Woods (see sections 3.1.2 and 3.1.3) were trying to approximate. However, in their formalization of the problem K&L are aiming for higher things, namely a solution for the general problem of definite reference, from which an anaphor resolver will fall out as an immediate corollary. I believe their model however still represents less than the minimum equipment for a successful solution to the problem. For example (as K&L themselves point out) their model cannot handle examples like (2-106)[12] where determining the reference relationship requires inference. Further, as we shall soon see, the model of focus as a simple shift register is overly simplistic.[13]

---

[10]In general, we will mean by the FOCUS of a point in text all concepts and entities from the preceding text that are referable at that point. As should soon be clear, focus is just what we have been calling "consciousness".

[11]In Hirst (1976b), I proposed that their model really requires three other focus sets — locative, verbal and actional — for the resolution of locative, pro-verbial and proactional anaphors, respectively.

[12](2-106) "It's nice having dinner with candles, but there's something funny about the two we've got tonight", Carol said. "They were the same length when you first lit them. Look at them now."
John chuckled. "The girl did say one would burn for four hours and the other for five", he replied . . .

[13]K&L have since developed their model to eliminate some of these problems, and we will see their later work in section 5.5. My reason for presenting their earlier work here is that it serves as a useful conceptual scaffold from which to build both our review of traditional anaphora resolution methods and our exposition of modern methods.

3.2.2. Syntax methods

Linguists have found many syntactic constraints on pronominalization in sentence generation. These can be used to eliminate otherwise acceptable antecedents in resolution fairly easily. We will look at a couple of examples:[14]

The most obvious constraint is REFLEXIVIZATION. Consider:

(3-19) Nadia says that Sue is knitting a sweater for <u>her</u>.

Her is Nadia or, in the right context, some other female, but cannot be Sue, as English syntax requires the reflexive *herself* to be used if Sue is the intended referent. In general an anaphoric NP is coreferential with the subject NP of the same simple sentence if and only if the anaphor is reflexive.

Another constraint prohibits a pronoun in a main clause referring to an NP in a subsequent subordinate clause:

(3-20) Because Ross slept in, <u>he</u> was late for work.

(3-21) Because <u>he</u> slept in, Ross was late for work.

(3-22) Ross was late for work because <u>he</u> slept in.

(3-23) <u>He</u> was late for work because Ross slept in.

In the first three sentences, *he* and *Ross* can be coreferential. In (3-23), however, *he* cannot be Ross because of the above constraint, and either *he* is someone in the wider context of the sentence or the text is ill-formed.

We have already seen that syntax-based methods by themselves are not enough. However, syntax-oriented methods may still play a role in anaphora resolution, as we saw in section 3.1.6.

> *The fool hath said in his heart,*
> *There is no God.*
> — *David*[15]

3.2.3. The heuristic approach

This is where prejudices start showing. Many AI workers, myself included, adhere to the maxim "One good theory is worth a thousand heuristics". People like Yorick Wilks (1971, 1973a, 1973b, 1975c) would disagree, arguing that language by its very nature — its lack of a sharp boundary — does not always allow (or perhaps NEVER allows) the formation of "100%-correct" theories; language understanding cannot be an exact science, and therefore heuristics will always be needed to plug the gaps. If the heuristic approach has failed so

---

[14]See Langacker (1969) and Ross (1969) for more syntactic restrictions on pronominalization.

[15]*Psalms* 14:1.

far, so this viewpoint says, then we just haven't found the right heuristics.[16]

While not totally rejecting Wilks's arguments,[17] I believe that the search for a good theory on anaphora resolution should not yet be terminated and labelled a failure. Gathering heuristics may suffice for the construction of a particular practical system, such as LSNLIS, but the aim of present work is to find more general principles. (Chapter 5 describes several theoretical approaches to the problem.)

This does not mean that we have no time for heuristics. The essence of our quest is COMPLETENESS. Thus, a taxonomy of anaphors or coreferences, together with an algorithm which will recognize each and apply a heuristic to resolve it, would be acceptable if it could be shown to handle every case the English language has to offer. And indeed, if we were to develop the heuristic approach, this would be our goal.[18]

However, our prospects for reaching this goal appear dismal. Consider first the problem of a taxonomy of anaphors, coreferences and definite references. Halliday and Hasan (1976), in attempting to classify different usages in their study of cohesion in English, identify 26 distinct types which can function in 29 distinct ways. (Compare my loose and informal classification in section 2.3.15.) While it is possible that some of their categories can be combined in a taxonomy useful for computational understanding of text, it is equally likely that as many, if not more, of their categories will need further subdivision. There is, moreover, no way yet of ensuring completeness in such a taxonomy, nor of ensuring that a heuristic will work properly on all applicable cases.

Also, there is the problem of semantics again. Rules which will allow the resolution of anaphors like those of the following examples will require either a further fragmentation of the taxonomy, or a fragmentation within the heuristic for each category:

> (3-24) When Sue went to Nadia's home for dinner, she served sukiyaki au gratin.
>
> (3-25) When Sue went to Nadia's home for dinner, she ate sukiyaki au gratin.

(These examples will be referred to collectively below as the 'sukiyaki' examples.) Here she, superficially ambiguous, means Nadia in (3-24) and Sue in (3-25).

Thus, a heuristic approach will essentially degenerate into a demon-like system (Charniak 1972), in which each heuristic is just a demon watching out for its own special case. Although this is theoretically fine, the shortcomings of such systems are well-known (Charniak 1976).

---

[16] For a discussion of Wilks's arguments in detail, see Hirst (1976a).

[17] I confess that when in a slough of despond I sometimes fear he may be right.

[18] One attempt at the heuristic approach was made by Baranofsky (1970), who described such a taxonomy with appropriate algorithms. However, her heuristics made no attempt to be complete, but rather to cover a wide range with as few cases as possible. I have been unable to determine whether the heuristics were ever implemented in a computer program.

3.2.3 The heuristic approach

All this is not to do away with heuristics entirely. As Wilks points out, we may be forced to use them to plug up holes in any theory, and, moreover, any theory may contain one or more layers of heuristics.[19]

3.2.4. The case grammar approach

Case "grammars" (Fillmore 1968, 1977), with their wide theoretical base, are able to resolve many anaphors in a way that is perhaps more simple and elegant than heuristics. The extra information provided by cases is often sufficient to easily pair reference with referent, given the meaning of the words involved.

For example, this approach is able to handle differences in the meaning of a word or anaphor in context. Compare (3-26) and (3-27):

(3-26) Ross asked Daryel to hold his books for a minute.

(3-27) Ross asked Daryel to hold his breath for a minute.

In the first sentence, *his* refers to Ross, the default referent,[20] and in the second, it refers to Daryel. Further, in each sentence, *hold* has a different meaning — *support* and *retain* respectively[21] — and handling the difference would be difficult for many systems. A case-driven parser, such as Taylor's (1975) (see section 3.1.5), would have a dictionary entry for each meaning of *hold*. In this example, *breath* could only pass the tests associated with the case-frame for one meaning, while *books* could only pass the tests for the other. Hence the correct meaning would be chosen. It is then possible to resolve the anaphors. In (3-26), there is nothing to contraindicate the assignment of the default. In (3-27), the system could determine that since the *retain* sense of *hold* was chosen, *his* must refer to Daryel. Taylor's parser does not have this resolution capability, but to program it would be fairly straightforward, if a default finder could be given.

Case-based systems also have an advantage in the resolution of situational anaphors. Compare (2-40)[22] with (3-28):

---

[19] You may have noticed that most of my arguments in this section depend on precisely what I mean by a "heuristic", and that I have placed it somewhere on a continuum between "theory" and "demon". While this is not the place to discuss this matter in detail, I am using the word to mean one of a set of essentially uncoordinated rules of thumb which together suffice to provide a method of achieving an end under a variety of conditions.

[20] Some idiolects appear not to accept this default, and see the anaphor as ambiguous.

[21] That these two uses of *hold* are not the same is demonstrated by the following examples:

(i) Daryel held his books and his briefcase.

(ii) ?Daryel held his books and his breath.

[22] (2-40) The president was shot while riding in a motorcade down a major Dallas boulevard today; it caused a panic on Wall Street.

(3-28) The president was shot while riding in a motorcade down a major Dallas boulevard today; it was crowded with spectators at the time.

A general heuristic system would have trouble detecting the difference between the *it* in each case. A case grammar approach can use the properties of the verb forms *to be crowded* and *to cause* to recognize that in (2-40) the referent may be situational. To determine exactly what situation is being referred to, though, some UNDERSTANDING of sentences will be needed. This problem doesn't arise in this particular example, since there is only one previous situation that can be referenced prosentientially. But as we have seen, whole paragraphs and chapters can be prosentientially referenced, and deciding which previous sentence, or group of sentences is intended is a task which requires use of meaning.

The case approach would not be sufficient to resolve our 'sukiyaki' examples. Recall (3-24).[23] The parser would look for a referent for *she* with such conditions as MUST-BE HUMAN, MUST-BE FEMALE and SHOULD-BE HOST. But how is it to know that Nadia, and not Sue, is the item to be preferred as a HOST? Humans know this from the location of the event taking place. However, a case-driven parser does not have this knowledge, expressed in the subordinate clause at the start of the sentence, available to it. To get this information, an inferencing mechanism is needed to determine from the verb *went* that the serving took place at, or on the way to,[24] Nadia's home, and to infer that therefore Nadia is probably the host. Such an inferencer will also need to use a database of information from previous sentences, as not all the knowledge necessary for resolution need be given in the one sentence at hand. (For example, in this case the sentence may be broken into two simple sentences.) This database must contain semantic information — meanings of, and inferences from, past sentences; that is, sentences must be, in some sense, UNDERSTOOD.[25] Thus we see once more that parsing with anaphor resolution cannot take place without understanding.

Now consider (3-25).[26] Here, a case approach has even less information — only MUST-BE ANIMATE and MUST-BE FEMALE — and no basis for choosing between Sue and Nadia as the subject of the main clause. The way we know that it is Sue is that she is the topic of the preceding subordinate clause and, in the absence of any indication to the contrary, the topic remains unchanged. Notice that this rule is neither syntactic nor semantic but pragmatic — a convention of conversation and writing. Apart from this, there is no other way of determining that Sue, and not Nadia, is the sukiyaki consumer in question.

---

[23](3-24) When Sue went to Nadia's home for dinner, she served sukiyaki au gratin.

[24] Sentence (i) shows that we cannot conclude from the subordinate clause that the location of the action expressed in subsequent verbs necessarily takes place at Nadia's home:

    (i) When Sue went to Nadia's home for dinner, she caught the wrong bus and arrived an hour late.

[25]The database will also need common-sense real-world knowledge.

[26](3-25) When Sue went to Nadia's home for dinner, she ate sukiyaki au gratin.

3.2.4 The case grammar approach

Another use of cases is in METAPHOR resolution for anaphor resolution. A system which uses a network of cases in conjunction with a network of concept associations to resolve metaphoric uses of words has been constructed by Roger Browse (1977, 1978). For example, it can understand that in:

(3-29) Ross drank the bottle.

what was drunk was actually the contents of the bottle. This is determined from the knowledge that bottles contain fluid, and *drink* requires a fluid object. Such metaphor resolution can be necessary in anaphor resolution, especially where the anaphor is metaphoric but its antecedent isn't, or vice versa. For example:

(3-30) Ross picked up the bottle and drank <u>it</u>.

(3-31) Ross drank the bottle and threw <u>it</u> away.

We can conclude from this discussion that a case-base is not enough, but a maintenance of focus (possibly by means of heuristics) and an understanding of what is being parsed are essential. We have also seen that cases can aid resolution of metaphoric anaphors and anaphoric metaphors.

How could such a case system resolve paraphrase coreferences and definite reference? Clearly, case information alone is inadequate, and will need assistance from some other method. Nevertheless, we see that a case "grammar" may well serve as a firm base for anaphora resolution.

3.2.5. Analysis by synthesis

Transformational grammarians have spent considerable time pondering the problem of where pronouns and other surface proforms come from, and have produced a number of theories which I will not attempt to discuss here. This leads to the possibility of anaphora resolution through analysis by synthesis, where we start out with an hypothesized deep structure which is generated by intelligent (heuristic?) guesswork, and apply transformational rules to it until we either get the required surface or fail.

What this involves is a parser, such as the ATN parser of Woods (1970), to provide a deep structure with anaphors intact. Then each anaphor is replaced by a hypothesis as to its referent, and transformations are applied to see if the same surface is generated. If so, the hypotheses are accepted; otherwise new ones are tried. The hypotheses are presumably selected by a heuristic search.

There are many problems with this method. First, the generation of a surface sentence is a nondeterministic process which may take a long time, especially if exhaustive proof of failure is needed; a large number of combinations of hypotheses may compound this further. Second, this approach does not take into account meanings of sentences, let alone the context of whole paragraphs or world knowledge. For example, in (3-32):

(3-32) Sue visited Nadia for dinner because <u>she</u> invited <u>her</u>.

both the hypotheses *she = Sue, her = Nadia* and *she = Nadia, her = Sue* could be validated by this method and without recourse to world knowledge there is no way of deciding which is correct. Third, the method cannot handle intersentential anaphora. We must conclude that analysis by synthesis is not promising.

3.2.6. Resolving anaphors by inference

If we are to bring both world knowledge and word meaning to bear in anaphora resolution, then some inferencing mechanism which operates in this domain is needed. Possible paradigms for this include Rieger's Conceptual Memory (1975) (see 3.1.4) and Wilks's preference semantics (1973b, 1975a, 1975b) (see section 3.1.7).

Although conceptual dependency, which Conceptual Memory uses, is not without its problems (Davidson 1976), it may be possible to extend it for use in anaphor resolution. This would require giving it a linguistic interface such that reasoning which involves world knowledge, sentence semantics and the surface structure can be performed together – clearly pure inference, as in Conceptual Memory, is not enough. An effective method for representing and deploying world knowledge will also be needed. A system using FRAMES (Minsky 1975), or SCRIPTS (Schank and Abelson 1975, 1977) (which are essentially a subset of frames), appears promising. Frames allow the use of world knowledge to develop EXPECTATIONS about an input, and to interpret it in light of these. For instance, in the 'sukiyaki' examples, the mention of Sue visiting Nadia's home should invoke a VISITING frame, in which the expectation that Nadia might serve Sue food would be generated, after which the resolution of the anaphor is a matter of easy inference.

In Wilks's system inference is more controlled than in Conceptual Memory; whereas the latter searches for as many inferences to make as it can without regard to their possible use,[27] the former tries to find the shortest possible inference chain to achieve its goal. Although Wilks's system does not use the concept of expectations, its use of preferred situations can achieve much the same ends. In the 'sukiyaki' examples, the host would be the preferred server.

---

[27]Rieger has since developed a more controlled approach to inference generation (Rieger 1978).

3.2.7. Summary and discussion

I have discussed in this section five different approaches to anaphor resolution. They are:

1 syntactic methods − which are clearly insufficient;

2 heuristics − which we decided may be necessary, though we would like to minimize their inelegant presence, preferring as much theory as possible;

3 case grammars − which we saw to be elegant and powerful, but not powerful enough by themselves to do all we would like done;

4 analysis by synthesis − which looks like a dead loss; and

5 inference − which seems to be an absolute necessity to use world knowledge, but which must be heavily controlled to prevent unnecessary explosion.

From this it seems that an anaphor resolver will need just about everything it can lay its hands on − case knowledge, inference, world knowledge, and word meaning to begin with, not to mention the mechanisms for focus determination, discourse analysis, etc that I will discuss in subsequent chapters, and perhaps some of the finer points of surface syntax too.[28]

---

[28]That a boots-and-all approach is necessary should perhaps have been clear from the earliest attempts in this area because of the very nature of language. For natural language was designed (if I may be so bold as to suggest a high order of teleology in its evolution) for communication between human beings, and it follows that no part of language is beyond the limits of competence of the normal human mind. And it is not unreasonable to expect, a fortiori, that no part is far behind the limits of competence either, for if it were, either it could not meet the need for a high degree of complexity in our communication, or else language use would be a tediously simplistic task requiring long texts to communicate short facts.

Consider our own problem, anaphora. Imagine what language would be like if we did not have this device to shorten repeated references to the same thing, and to aid perception of discourse cohesion. Clearly, anaphora is a highly desirable component of language. It is hardly surprising then that language should take advantage of all our intellectual abilities to anaphorize whenever it is intellectually possible for a listener to resolve it. Hence, any complete NLU system will need just about the full set of human intellectual abilities to succeed. (See also Rieger (1975:268).)

Chapter 4

THE NEED FOR DISCOURSE THEME IN ANAPHORA RESOLUTION

The procedure is actually quite simple. First you arrange things into different groups depending on their makeup. Of course, one pile may be sufficient, depending on how much there is to do. If you have to go somewhere else due to lack of facilities that is the next step, otherwise you are pretty well set. It is important not to overdo any particular endeavour. That is, it is better to do too few things at once than too many.

— John D Bransford and Marcia K Johnson (1973)[1]

In this chapter, we bring two more factors, which are interrelated, into play:

1 focus, and

2 discourse theme and discourse pragmatics.

In section 3.2.1 we introduced formally the concept of a focus set to model consciousness as a repository for antecedents, and we noted that the approaches described in section 3.1 do not explicitly use focus, but instead rely on a simple kind of history list to retain possible referents. In this and the following chapters we will consider in detail the problems entailed in focus:

1 Is an explicit focus really necessary?

2 What does focus look like? Is it just a set, or has it more structure than that?

3 How is focus maintained? What makes entities enter and leave focus?

We will also introduce the notion of discourse theme and ask ourselves:

1 Does an anaphor resolver need to use discourse theme?

2 How is theme related to focus?

3 How is theme determined?

---

[1]A paragraph said to have no theme, used in their experiments. Subjects found it very hard to comprehend or recall until it was given a theme by adding the heading *Washing Clothes*.

4.1. Discourse theme

To define the theme of a discourse, we appeal to the intuition as follows: The
THEME or TOPIC of a discourse is the main entity or concept that the discourse is
ABOUT — the subject central to the ideas expressed in the text, "the idea(s) at
the forefront of the speaker's mind" (Allerton 1978:134). We use this intuitive
definition because no more rigorously formal one is yet agreed on upon in
linguistics.

A simple example: Is (4-1):

(4-1) The boy is riding the horse.

a statement about the boy or the horse? In this case, the answer seems to be
clearly the former; *the boy* is the topic and *is riding the horse* is a comment
about the topic.[2] As we shall see, however, the choice is not always as clear-cut
as this. Much work has been done in attempting to capture precisely the concept of theme, and attempting to determine rules for deciding what the theme
of a given text is. (See for example the papers in Li (1975).)

Let us begin by sorting out our terminology. To the confusion of all,
different workers have used different nomenclatures, often describing the same
concept with different words, or different concepts with the same words. I
suspect that the failure of some people working in the field to realize that they
and their colleagues were not talking the same language has hindered progress
in this area. The following table summarizes terminology used:[3]

The boy	is riding the horse	Used by
topic	comment	Sgall et al (1973)
theme	rheme	Halliday (1967)
old	new	Chafe (1970)
given	new	Haviland and Clark (1974), Clark and Haviland (1977), and Allerton (1978)
logical subject	logical object[4]	Chomsky (1965)
focus	—	Sidner (1978a, 1978b)
psychological subject	psychological predicate	Hornby (1972)

---

[2]This is not the case in all contexts. If (4-1) were the answer to (i):

(i) Who is riding the horse?

then *the boy* would be the comment and *riding the horse* the topic.

[3]While the words in each column describe closely related concepts, it should not be inferred
that they are precisely synonymous. In particular, Halliday (1967) and Allerton (1978) draw a
distinction between theme and old, and between rheme and new (see section 4.1.1).

(See Allerton (1978) for a more detailed discussion of terminological confusion.)

In this thesis I will follow Allerton (1978) and use the words *theme* and *topic* interchangeably; but I will also need to make a distinction not yet commonly recognized explicitly in the nomenclature jungle: I will use LOCAL THEME or LOCAL TOPIC to refer to what a SENTENCE is about, and GLOBAL THEME or GLOBAL TOPIC to refer to what a DISCOURSE is about at a given point. These two concepts often coincide, but frequently don't. For example, in (4-2):

> (4-2) Nadia's chinchilla is shaped like a pear with a brush for a tail. Its teeth are long, but not very sharp.

the local and global topics of the first sentence are both *Nadia's chinchilla*. In the second sentence the global theme is unchanged from the first sentence, while the local theme is now *Nadia's chinchilla's teeth*.

There are currently two major paradigms in investigating problems of discourse theme. The theoretical approach, initially centred in Europe, uses introspective linguistic analysis, and is typified by the work of Firbas (1964), Sgall, Hajičová and Benešová (1973), Halliday (1967), Chafe (1970, 1972, 1975) and many of the papers in Li (1975). The experimental approach uses the techniques of psycholinguistics, and is typified by the work of Hornby (1971, 1972) and Johnson-Laird (1968a, 1968b). First we will look at each paradigm in turn, and then at their applications in computational analysis of language.

4.1.1. The linguistic approach

Chafe (1970:210-233, 1972) discusses the relationship between the topic of a sentence and the information in it which is not new. For example, in (4-1), it is assumed that the boy is already being talked about, and is therefore the topic, while the new information conveyed is what the boy is doing, riding the horse, and this is therefore the comment. Chafe describes given, or old, information as that already "in the air", used as a starting point for the addition of further information. Old information need not be explicitly spoken;[5] it may be something assumed to be known to both speaker and listener. For example, if I come up to you and say (4-3):

---

[4] *The horse* rather than *is riding the horse* is the logical object in Chomsky's nomenclature.

[5] A common literary device, for example, is to begin a novel with a sentence that presumes information, forcing the reader to immediately construct a mental frame containing this information, thereby plunging them straight into the story.

A similar phenomenon occurs when sentences are presented in a contextual vacuum, as are most of the example texts in this thesis. A series of experiments by Haviland and Clark (1974) showed that people take longer to comprehend sentences which presume ungiven information, implying that time is taken to create or invoke the mental frame required to understand the sentence.

(4-3) Hi! Did you hear that Ross was arrested on a morals charge?

it is assumed that we both know who Ross is. If I added the word *again*, it is also assumed we know about his previous arrest, and the new information that I am giving you is that it happened once more.

Halliday (1967) and Allerton (1978) refine the concept thus: given is what was being spoken about before, while theme is what is being spoken about now, these not necessarily being the same thing.

The concept of theme has been generalized somewhat by Chafe (1972) to that of FOREGROUNDING; if the topic is what is "in the air", then foregrounded items are those "on stage"; they are those "assumed to be in the hearer's consciousness" (Chafe 1972:50, 1974). When a lexical item occurs in a discourse, it automatically becomes foregrounded in future occurrences, says Chafe, until it retreats to the wings through lack of further mention. How long this retreat takes is unclear, and probably varies depending on other items taking the places, or "slots", of previous ones. Clearly, foregrounding is very similar to what we have been calling focusing.

In verbal discourse, a lexical item is signalled as being the theme or as being in the foreground by vocal tone, stress and gesture, as well as by textual devices. We see in (4-4) and (4-5) that the comment is stressed and the theme is not:

(4-4)   What is Nadia doing?
        Nadia is PRACTISING ACUPUNCTURE.
        *NADIA is practising acupuncture.

(4-5)   Who is practising acupuncture?
        NADIA is practising acupuncture.
        *Nadia is PRACTISING ACUPUNCTURE.

In written language the topic is usually indicated by syntactic, semantic and pragmatic cues, though italics or upper case may be used to simulate vocal stress.

We see, then, that the linguistic approach assumes that we have an intuitive idea of what topic is, and tries to formulate rules to formalize this idea. It has, however, yet to agree on any precise definition of theme, or produce any formal method for determining the theme of a sentence or discourse by computational analysis.

4.1.2. The psycholinguistic approach

To determine what subjects THOUGHT the theme of a sentence was, Hornby (1971, 1972) used the following experimental procedure: A number of pairs of pictures were drawn with each picture having three components, two objects and an action. The action was the same in each of the pair. A typical pair showed *(a)* an Indian building a tepee and *(b)* an Eskimo building an igloo. For each pair, subjects were presented with sentences which described each picture with partial correctness. For the above pair, typical sentences were (4-6) and (4-7):

> (4-6) The Indian is building the igloo.
>
> (4-7) The one who is building the igloo is the Indian.

Subjects were asked to pick which picture each stimulus sentence "is about, even though it is not exactly correct" (1972:637). In the above example, most felt that (4-6) was nearest to *(a)* and (4-7) to *(b)*. The component that is the same in both picture and sentence (here, Indian and igloo respectively) is then assumed to be the psychological subject, or local theme.

Hornby found that the theme of a sentence is not necessarily either the syntactic subject or the first item mentioned, a result contrary to suggestions that word order determines theme (Halliday 1967) or that case relationships play a role independent of surface syntax (Fillmore 1968).

4.1.3. Lacunae abounding

Although much work has been done in the area of theme, there is little of substance to use. The linguistic approach has served to intuitively define for us the concepts of theme and foreground, but has given us no way to find them in a text, even though, as we will see, finding them is a necessity in NLU. Similarly, the psycholinguistic approach has so far shown us where not to look for rules about theme, but has not helped us find them.

I believe that Hornby's experiments point us in the right direction: the theme of a sentence is a function of, inter alia, both its construction and the case relationships therein, and, if in a context, then of the topic of the previous sentence as well. It therefore remains to find this function. From this should follow rules for the foreground, which we can use in deciding when things no longer remain in focus. Despite the simplicity with which it can be stated, this goal is, of course, a major research problem. In the next chapter we will look at some recent approaches to it.

4.2. Why focus and theme are needed in anaphor resolution

Is a recency list really inadequate as a focus for anaphor resolution? Does discourse theme really play a role? In this section I will show that the answer to both these questions is "yes".

Taking an opposing view, Yorick Wilks (1975b) rejects the use of theme, except as a last resort, on the basis of the following examples:

(4-8) John left the window and drank the wine on the table. It was good.

(4-9) John left the window and drank the wine on the table. It was brown and round.

(These examples, together with (4-10), will be referred to below as the 'table' examples.) In (4-8), *it* clearly refers to the wine. In (4-9), things are not so clear; Wilks says that *it* must mean the table, and, uncoincidentally, the anaphor resolution component of his natural language system comes to the same conclusion, using the method of "preference semantics" (see section 3.1.7), whereby the table is chosen as the referent on the grounds that it is much more likely to be brown and round than the window or the wine. Since the wine (but not the table) is the theme here, Wilks concludes that we can therefore "reject all simple solutions based on [theme]"[6] (1975b:68).

The problem is that Wilks's interpretation of the sentence is wrong, or at best idiolectic. In my idiolect, (4-9) could only be describing the wine as brown and round (adjectives which make as much sense as many of the other terms often applied to wine).[7] Informants, speakers of American and Australian English, agreed. One described (4-9) as an absurdity, and when told that *it* meant the table replied that that possibility had not even occurred to them. When I included (4-9) in a conference presentation (Hirst 1977a), the audience laughed at it. Clearly, (4-9) is ill-formed.[8]

Example (4-9) is ill-formed because when *it* is encountered in the text, *the table* is no longer in focus; that is, it cannot be referred to anaphorically,

---

[6]The word in brackets was originally *focus*; where Wilks uses this term, he apparently means *discourse theme, topic*, or *focus of attention*. To avoid confusion with our sense of the word *focus*, I have amended this quotation.

[7]Compare Lehrer (1975), who showed that many oenological terms contain zero bits of information.

[8]This points out the danger, well known in linguistics but perhaps not in artificial intelligence, of losing one's intuition for even one's native language. (Spencer (1973) has shown that linguists have quite different intuitions regarding grammaticality and acceptability from non-linguists.) When generating sample sentences to demonstrate a point about the nature of language, it is surprisingly easy to come up with ill-formed or marginal sentences without being aware of the fact. (See also Carroll and Bever (1978), whose experiments suggest that linguistic intuition varies with context and mental state, including degree of self-awareness.) It is therefore advisable to at least test examples on informants (namely, long-suffering non-linguist friends) before using them. I have done this with important and/or contentious examples in this thesis, but nevertheless do not believe that I am necessarily innocent of generating ill-formed sentences myself. This is why I have, throughout this thesis, where possible, taken my examples from "real-world text", and given a complete citation of the source. Nevertheless, real-world text is sometimes suspect — people inadvertently write sentences they themselves would not accept, and some people are just plain illiterate — and in some instances I have marked real-world text used in this thesis as ill-formed when it grated my idiolect. (In section 7.3, I address the question of better alternatives for obtaining or testing linguistic data.)

A related problem is that of idiolects. Some examples in this thesis were acceptable to some but not all informants (all such examples are so noted). I concede that my difference here with Wilks may be merely idiolectic; however, his idiolect appears to be in a small minority (not that that proves anything).

4.2 Why focus and theme are needed in anaphor resolution

notwithstanding that only a period separates it from the *it*. (We will see in section 5.1.2 an explanation of why this happens.) Clearly, an anaphor resolver with nothing more than a history list ordered by recency would fail to find (4-9) ill-formed;[9] a similar language generator could erroneously produce it. Moreover, the recency-list approach would spuriously consider (4-10) ambiguous, though it isn't:

(4-10) John picked up the toy on the table. It was made of wood.

and then choose the wrong "possibility", namely the table being wooden, on grounds of greater recency and equal reasonableness.

To show that the argument above does not rest solely on the idiolectic acceptability or not of (4-9), here is another example:

(4-11) If an incendiary bomb drops near you, don't lose your head. Put it in a bucket and cover it with sand.[10]

There are only two candidates for the first *it* here: *an incendiary bomb* and *your head*. Semantics and world knowledge indicate the former, as its speaker presumably intended, yet the latter unambiguously "sounds like" the correct referent despite the nonsense resulting; and therein lies the jest. That *your head* is the referent despite the presence of a better choice means that the better choice violated other constraints which prevented it even being considered as a candidate in the resolution. These constraints are those of focus: *an incendiary bomb* was not properly in focus at the time of the first *it* and therefore was not available. However, *your head* appears to be the topic of the sentence despite the need to fracture the idiomatic expression, and is ipso facto the "dominant" item in focus.[11] When presented with (4-11), Wilks's preference semantics program would not, I think, see the humour, but would wrongly choose the bomb as the referent of *it*.

The above discussion demonstrates that focus is an integral part of language (or at least of English). Any anaphora resolution system should therefore take it into account; failure to do so will result in the wrong answers.

A second reason for maintaining a focus is that without it the number of possible referents grows with the length of the text. Clearly an NLU system

---

[9]An important point relevant here is the comprehension of ill-formed sentences: humans can do it in many cases, and it is desirable for computer natural language understanders to do so too. Baranofsky (1970), for example, gave heuristics for resolving the relative pronoun in sentences such as (i):

(i) *A man went to the fair who lost his mind.

Wilks might therefore defend his system as one which has the bonus advantage of understanding ill-formed sentences. But then he could not reject theme-based resolution on the basis of (4-9). In addition, we surely want such a system to try all possible well-formed interpretations first, and flag a sentence for which it is forced to make an assumption of ill-formedness.

[10]This text is of obscure origin, but is usually alleged to have come from a British air raid precautions leaflet during World War II.

[11]See section 5.1 for support for this assertion.

attempting to read a scientific paper, for example, should not, on the fourth page, look back over all entities evoked by the entire preceding text for the most reasonable antecedent for an anaphor. But, as should be clear by now, a simple shift register, saving the last n possible antecedents or those from the last n sentences, is not enough.

We now agree that focus is necessary. The following examples demonstrate that discourse THEME plays a role in focus:

(4-12) Nadia hastily swallowed the licorice, and followed Ross to the bathroom. She stared in disbelief at the water coming out of the tap; it was black.

Wilks's preference semantics system will (as far as I can determine from his 1975b paper) choose *licorice* over *water* as the referent of *it*, because licorice is more likely than water to be black. The licorice should have been discarded from focus by the end of the first sentence of (4-12). It is out of focus because it is unrelated to the discourse topic or theme, the strange events in the bathroom, at the point the anaphor occurs.

Now consider this text, from *Wheels*,[12] in which the president of General Motors discusses with his wife charges brought against the motor industry by Vale, a Ralph Nader—like character:

(4-13) She continued, unperturbed, "Mr Vale quotes the Bible about air pollution."
"For Christ's sake! Where does the Bible say anything about that?"
"Not Christ's sake, dear. It's in the Old Testament."
His curiosity aroused, he growled. "Go ahead, read it. You intended to, anyway."
"From Jeremiah," Coralie said. "'And I brought you into a plentiful country, to eat the fruit thereof and the goodness thereof; but when ye entered ye defiled my land, and made mine heritage an abomination.'" She poured more coffee for them both. "I do think that's rather clever of him."

Vale is still available to Coralie in her conversation as an antecedent for "him" after eight intervening sentences of the conversation, and her anaphor is quite comprehensible to us in the written report of the conversation, despite ten intervening sentences which contain two other possible referents – the president of General Motors and Jeremiah. This is possible because Mr Vale and his quotation is the topic of the whole conversation. It may be objected that there is no possible confusion – Vale is the only referent for *him* that makes sense; in particular, Coralie would not refer to her husband in the third person when addressing him. But as we saw with (4-9) and (4-11), "making sense" is not enough. In any case, it is non-trivial to exclude the interpretation in which *him* means Jeremiah, and Coralie is commenting on something like the clever

---

[12]Hailey, Arthur. *Wheels*. New York, 1971, page 2. Quoted by Hobbs (1977).

4.2 Why focus and theme are needed in anaphor resolution

use of language in the quotation. It is also apparent that the reference is to Mr Vale as a concept in consciousness rather than the words *Mr Vale*, which are almost certainly forgotten by the reader by the time the reference occurs.

Here is another example of reference to discourse topic:

> (4-14) *Dear Ann:* No lectures on morality, please, I'm not asking you whether or not I should continue to sleep with this man. I have already decided that he is better than nothing. Now to the problem:
>
> The guy's toenails are like razor blades. I get up some mornings and feel like I've been stabbed. I have mentioned this to him a few times, but he does nothing about it. I need help. — CLAWED-A-PLENTY
>
> *Answer:* Buy King Kong a pair of toenail scissors. Be extra generous and offer to trim <u>them</u> for him. If he refuses, insist that he sleep with his socks on — or move to another bed.[13]

Them is the toenails in question, the topic of the second and third paragraphs, but not the actual text *the guy's toenails*, which is too far back to be recalled word for word. Nor is *them* a strained anaphor into *toenail scissors*, as the reference is ill-formed if the first two sentences of the answer are taken out of context. (In passing, we also notice in (4-14) the epithet *King Kong*, which requires a large amount of world knowledge and inference to recognize and comprehend.)

Lastly, consider this text:

> (4-15) The winning species would have a greater amount of competitive ability than the loser as far as that resource axis of the n-dimensional niche is concerned (e.g. <u>it</u> would be more adapted to using that resource in that particular habitat).[14]

Not only is *the winning species* the local theme and the antecedent of *it*, but it is the only item in focus. None of the more recent NPs — *a greater amount*, *a greater amount of competitive ability*, *competitive ability*, *the loser*, *that resource axis*, *the n-dimensional niche*, *that resource axis of the n-dimensional niche* — can be referred to by this *it* regardless of the text that follows it. That is, there is NO text which could replace the text after *it* in (4-15) and make a well-formed sentence in which *it* refers to one of the more recent NPs.[15]

---

[13]From: Landers, Ann. [Advice column]. *The Vancouver sun*, 11 August 1976, page B5.

[14]From: Mares, M A. Observation of Argentine desert rodent ecology, with emphasis on water relations of *eligmodontia typus*. in: I Prakash and P K Ghosh (editors). *Rodents in desert environments* (= Monographiae biologicae *26*). The Hague: Dr W Junk b v Publishers, 1975.

[15]For support for this type of assertion, see section 5.6.

4.2 Why focus and theme are needed in anaphor resolution

4.3. Can focusing be tamed?

Implicit in the preceding discussion is the assumption that given any point in a text there is a set of focus sets associated with that point. It should be clear from our exposition so far that this is indeed the case. What is not so clear is how we can know the contents of these focus sets. For example, if the point is a pronoun, P, we are interested in knowing the contents of the nominal focus set F_n, which consists of all those concepts that P could refer to for some following text. More formally, F_n is a function of P and the preceding text t defined by:

(4-16) $Fn(t,P) = \{n \mid n$ is a noun phrase contained in t, or a concept evoked by t, and there exists t' such that tPt' is well-formed English text in which P refers to $n.\}$

At any given time, the nominal focus set F_n contains zero or more entities — foregrounded items — which are possible referents for anaphors. When a pronominally referent anaphor needs resolving, one of several cases can occur:

1 There is exactly one noun phrase in F_n which fits the basic syntactic and selectional constraints (see Chapter 6); it is chosen as the referent.

2 There are no suitable members of F_n; then either the alleged anaphor is really a cataphor or exophor, or the sentence is ill-formed.

3 There is more than one suitable member of F_n; then either *(a)* we need to choose one of these possibilities, or *(b)* the sentence is ambiguous.

Case *3(a)* is the one of most interest here. Many apparent ambiguities can be resolved by knowing what the topic is. We have already seen one example of this:

(4-17) Ross asked Daryel to hold his books for a minute.

This is unambiguous in most idiolects because the topic indicates that *his* means *Ross's*. In general, the present topic is the default referent, and this is why we would like to be able to determine the topic of a sentence.

The definition of F_n above is clearly not of much use computationally, as it begs the question: it assumes the anaphor resolution capability of which it is itself a part. Therefore, if we intend to make use of focusing, we will need other, easier, rules to determine the contents of the focus sets. It is likely that such rules exist — humans, after all, have no problems — but finding them may be difficult. However, we have no choice but to search.

Let's summarize: In this chapter, I have tried to show that focus and theme are necessary in anaphora resolution, and that they are closely related. In the next chapter, we will look at the nature of this relationship and at some attempts to discover rules for focus.

Chapter 5

DISCOURSE-ORIENTED ANAPHORA SYSTEMS AND THEORIES

It is indeed harmful to come under the sway of utterly new and strange doctrines.
    — *Confucius*[1]

The relationship between theme on the one hand and pronominalization, anaphora and reference in general on the other has often been noted — for example by Kuno (1975), Givón (1975), Hirst (1976b) and Hinds (1977). In this section we will look at some work which attempts to explicate and/or exploit this relationship in resolving anaphora.

5.1. Concept activatedness

Robert Kantor (1977) has investigated the problem of why some pronouns in discourse are more comprehensible than others, even when there is no ambiguity or anomaly. In Kantor's terms, a hard-to-understand pronoun is an example of INCONSIDERATE discourse, and speakers (or, more usually, writers) who produce such pronouns lack SECONDARY [LINGUISTIC] COMPETENCE. In our terms, an inconsiderate pronoun is one that is not properly in focus.

I will first summarize Kantor's work, and then discuss what we can learn about focus from it.

5.1.1. Kantor's thesis

Kantor's main exhibit is the following text:

(5-1) A good share of the amazing revival of commerce must be credited to the ease and security of communications within the empire. The Imperial fleet kept the Mediterranean Sea cleared of pirates. In each province, the Roman emperor repaired or constructed a number of skillfully designed roads. <u>They</u> were built for the army

---

[1]From: Ware, James R (translator). *The sayings of Confucius*. New York: Mentor, 1955.

but served the merchant class as well. Over them, messengers of the Imperial service, equipped with relays of horses, could average fifty miles a day.

He claims that the *they* in the penultimate sentence is hard to comprehend, and that most informants need to reread the previous text to find its referent. Yet the sentence is neither semantically anomalous nor ambiguous — *the roads* is the only plural NP available as a referent, and it occurs immediately before the pronoun with only a full-stop intervening (cf (4-9)). To explain this paradox is the task Kantor set himself.

Kantor's explanation is based on discourse topic and the listener's expectations. In (5-1), the discourse topic of the first three sentences is *easing and securing communication*. In the fourth sentence, there is an improper shift to the roads as the topic: improper, because it is unexpected, and there is no discourse cue to signal it. Had the demonstrative *these roads* been used, the shift would have been okay. (Note that a definite such as *the roads* is not enough.) Alternatively, the writer could have clarified the text by combining last three sentences with semicolons, indicating that the last two main clauses were to be construed as relating only to the preceding one rather than to the discourse as a whole.

Kantor identifies a continuum of factors affecting the comprehension of pronouns. At one end is UNRESTRICTED EXPECTATION and at the other NEGATIVE EXPECTATION. What this says in effect is that a pronoun is easy to understand if expected, and difficult if unexpected. This is not as vacuous as it at first sounds; Kantor provides an analysis of some subtle factors which affect expectation.

The most expected pronouns are those whose referent is the discourse topic, or something associated with it (though note the qualifications to this below). Consider:

(5-2) The final years of Henry's reign, as recorded by the admiring Hall, were given over to sport and gaiety, though there was little of the licentiousness that characterized the French court. The athletic contests were serious but very popular. Masques, jousts and spectacles followed one another in endless pageantry. He brought to Greenwich a tremendously vital court life, a central importance in the country's affairs, and above all, a great naval connection.[2]

In the last sentence, *he* is quite comprehensible, despite the distance back to its referent, because the discourse topic in all the sentences is *Henry's reign*. An example of the converse — an unexpected pronoun which is difficult despite recency — can be seen in (5-1) above. Between these two extremes are other cases involving references to aspects of the local topic, changes in topic, syntactic parallelism, and, in topicless instances, recency (though the effect of recency decays very fast). I will not describe these here; the interested reader

---

[2]From: Hamilton, Olive and Hamilton, Nigel. *Royal Greenwich*. Greenwich: The Greenwich

is referred to section 2.6.5 of Kantor's dissertation (1977).

Kantor then defines the notion of the ACTIVATEDNESS of a concept. This provides a continuum of concept givenness, which contrasts with the simple binary given-new distinction usually accepted in linguistics (for example Chafe (1970)). Kantor also distinguishes activatedness from the similar "communicative dynamism" of the Prague school (Firbas 1964). Activatedness is defined in terms of the comprehensibility phenomena described above: the more activated a concept is, the easier it is to understand an anaphoric reference to it. Thus activatedness depends upon discourse topic, context, and so forth.

5.1.2. The implications of Kantor's work

What are the ramifications of Kantor's thesis for focus? Clearly, the notions of activatedness and focus are very similar, though the latter has not previously been thought of as a continuum. It follows that the factors Kantor finds relevant for activatedness and comprehensibility of pronouns are also important for those of us who would maintain focus in computer-based NLU systems; we will have to discover discourse topic and topic shifts, generate pronominalization expectations, and so forth.

In other words, if we could dynamically compute (and maintain) the activatedness of each concept floating around, we would have a measure for the ordering of the focus set by preferability as referent — the referent for any given anaphor would be the most highly activated element which passes basic tests for number, gender and semantic reasonableness. And to find the activatedness of the concepts, we follow Kantor's pointers (which he himself concedes are very tenuous and difficult) to extract and identify the relevant factors from the text.

It may be objected that all we have done is produce a mere notational variant of the original problem. This is partly true. One should not gainsay the power of a good notation, however, and what we can buy here even with mere notational variance is the (perhaps limited, but non-zero) power of Kantor's investigations. And there is more to it than that. Previously, it has been thought that items either are in focus or they aren't, and that at each separate anaphor we need to compute a preference ranking of the focus elements for that anaphor. What Kantor tells us is that such a ranking exists independent of the actual use of anaphors in the text, and that we can find the ranking by looking at things like discourse topic.

Some miscellaneous comments on Kantor's work:

1 It can be seen as a generalization albeit a weakening of Grosz's (1977a, 1977b, 1978) findings on focus in task-oriented dialogues (where each sub-task becomes the new discourse topic, opening up a new set of possible referents), which are discussed below in section 5.2. (Kantor and Grosz were apparently

---

Bookshop, 1969. Quoted by Halliday and Hasan (1976:14), quoted by Kantor (1977).

unaware of each other's work; neither cites the other.)

2 It provides an explanation for focus problems that have previously baffled us. For example, in section 4.2 I contemplated the problem of the ill-formedness of this text:

(5-3) *John left the window and drank the wine on the table. It was brown and round.

I had previously (Hirst 1977a) thought this to be due to a syntactic factor — that cross-sentence pronominal reference to an NP in a relative clause or adjectival phrase qualifying an NP was not possible. However, it can also be explained as a grossly inconsiderate pronoun which does not refer to the topic properly — *the table* occurs only as a descriptor for the wine, and not as a concept in its own right. This would be a major restriction on possible reference to sub-aspects of topics.[3]

3 Kantor makes many claims about comprehensibility and the degree of well-formedness of sentences which others (as he concedes) may not agree with. He uses only himself (and his friends, sometimes) as an informant, and then only at an intuitive level.[4] Claims as strong and subtle as Kantor's cry out for empirical testing. Kieras (1978), to mention but one, has performed psycholinguistic experiments on the comprehensibility of paragraphs. Kantor's claims need verification by similar experiments. (Unfortunately, I myself am not in a position to do this.)[5]

5.2. Focus of attention in task-oriented dialogues

5.2.1. Motivation

Barbara Grosz (1977a, 1977b, 1978) studied the maintenance of the focus of attention in task-oriented dialogues and its effect on the resolution of definite reference, as part of SRI's speech understanding system project (Walker 1976, 1978). By a TASK-ORIENTED dialogue is meant one which has some single major well-defined task as its goal. For example, Grosz collected and studied dialogues in which an expert guides an apprentice in the assembly of an air compressor. She found that the structure of such dialogues parallels the

---

[3]Note however that this restriction may apply to all relative clauses and adjectival phrases. Then the syntactic explanation would still be correct and would be descriptively simpler.

[4]I do not deny that I am guilty too. But I at least try to do penance, in footnote 8 of Chapter 4 and in section 7.3. I also suggest that Kantor is more culpable than I, because of the peculiar subtlety of the phenomena he studied and because his results rely so heavily on his claims of well- and ill-formedness.

[5]Kantor tells me that he hopes to test some of his assertions by observing the eye movements of readers of considerate and inconsiderate texts, to find out if inconsiderate texts actually make readers physically search back for a referent.

structure of the task. That is, just as the major task is divided into several well-defined sub-tasks, and these perhaps into sub-sub-tasks and so on, the dialogue is likewise divided into sub-dialogues, sub-sub-dialogues, etc,[6] each corresponding to a task component, much as a well-structured Algol program is composed of blocks within blocks within blocks. As the dialogue progresses, each sub-dialogue in turn is performed in a strict depth-first order corresponding to the order of sub-task performance in the task goal (though note that some sub-tasks may not be ordered with respect to others). As we will see, this dialogue structure can be exploited in reference resolution.

Grosz's aim was to find ways of determining and representing the FOCUS OF ATTENTION of a discourse — that is, roughly speaking, its global theme and the things associated therewith — as a means for constraining the knowledge an NLU system needs to bring to bear in understanding discourse. In other words, the focus of attention is that knowledge which is relevant at a given point in a text for comprehension of the text.[7] Grosz claims that antecedents for definite reference can be found in the focus of attention. That is, the focus of attention is a superset of focus in our sense, the set of referable concepts (in this case definite reference, not just anaphoric reference). Moreover, no element in the focus of attention is excluded from being a candidate antecedent for a definite NP. Grosz thereby implies that all items in the focus of attention can be referred to, and that hence the two senses of the word *focus* are actually identical.

5.2.2. Representing and searching focus

In Grosz's representation, which uses a partitioned semantic net formalism (Hendrix 1975a, 1975b, 1978), an EXPLICIT FOCUS corresponds to a sub-dialogue, and includes, for each concept in it, type information about that concept and any situation in which that concept participates. For each item in the explicit focus, there is an associated IMPLICIT FOCUS, which includes subparts of objects in explicit focus, subevents of events in explicit focus, and participants in those subevents. The implicit focus attempts to account for reference to items that have a close semantic distance to items in focus (see sections 2.4.2 and 6.7), or which have a close enough relationship to items in focus to be able to be referred to (see section 2.4.2). The implicit focus is also used in detecting focus shifts (see below).

Then, at any given point in a text, antecedents of definite non-pronominal NPs can be found by searching through the explicit and implicit focus for a match for the reference. After checking the other non-pronominal NPs in the same sentence to see if the reference is intrasentential, the CURRENTLY ACTIVE

---

[6]Below I will use the prefix *sub-* generically to include *sub-sub-sub-*... to an indefinite level.

[7]In her later work (Grosz 1978), Grosz emphasizes focus*ing* as an active process carried out by dialogue participants.

explicit focus (the focus corresponding to the present sub-dialogue) is searched, and then if that search is not successful, the other currently open focus spaces (that is, those corresponding to sub-dialogues that the present sub-dialogue is contained in) are searched in order, back up to the top of the tree. As part of the search the implicit focus associated with each explicit focus is checked, as are subset relations, so that if a novel, say, is in focus, it could be referred to as *the book*. If there is still no success after this, one then checks whether the NP refers to a single unique concept (such as the sun), contains new information (such as *the red coat*, when a coat is in focus, but not yet known to be red), or refers to an item in implicit focus.

A similar search method could be used for pronouns. However, since pronouns carry much less information than other definite NPs, more inference is required by the reference matching process to disambiguate many syntactically ambiguous pronouns, and it would be necessary to search focus exhaustively, comparing reasonableness of candidate referents, rather than stopping at the first plausible one. In addition, other constraints on pronoun reference, such as local (rather than global) theme, and default referent, would also need to be taken into account; Grosz's mechanisms do not do this. However, Grosz does show how a partitioned network structure can be used to resolve certain types of ellipsis by means of syntactic and semantic pattern matching against the immediately preceding utterance, which may itself have been expanded from an elliptical expression. She leaves open for future research most of the problems in relating pronouns to focus.

5.2.3. Maintaining focus

Given this approach, one is then faced with the problem of deciding what the focus is at a given point in the discourse. For highly constrained task-oriented dialogues such as those Grosz considered, the question of an initial focus does not arise; it is, by definition, the overall task in question. The other component of the problem, handling changes and shifts in the focus, is attacked by Grosz in a top-down manner using the task structure as a guide.

A shift in focus can be indicated explicitly by an utterance, such as:

(5-4) Well, the reciprocating afterburner nozzle speed control is assembled. Next, it must be fitted above the preburner swivel hose cover guard cooling fin mounting rack.

In this case, the reciprocating afterburner nozzle speed control assembly sub-task and its corresponding sub-dialogue and focus are closed, and new ones are opened for the reciprocating afterburner nozzle speed control fitting, dominated by the same open sub-tasks/sub-dialogues/focuses in their respective trees that dominated the old ones. If however the new sub-task were a sub-task of the old one, then the old one would not be closed, but the new one added to the hierarchy below it as the new active focus space. The newly created focus space initially contains only those items referred to in the utterance, and those objects associated with the current sub-task. (Being ABLE to bring in the associated objects at this time is, of course, the crucial point on which the whole system relies.) As subsequent non-shift-causing utterances come in, their new information is added to the active focus space.

Usually, of course, speakers are not as helpful as in (5-4), and it is necessary to look for various clues to shifts in focus. For Grosz, the clues are definite NPs. If a definite NP from an utterance cannot be matched in focus, then this is a clue that the focus has shifted, and it is necessary to search for the new focus. If the antecedent of a definite NP is in the current implicit focus, this is a clue that a sub-task associated with this item is being opened. If the task structure is being followed, then the new focus will reflect the opening or closing of a sub-task.

Shifting cannot be done until a whole utterance is considered, as clues may conflict, or the meaning of the utterance may contraindicate the posited shift. In particular, recall that the task structure is only a guide, and does not define the dialogue structure absolutely. For example, the focus may shift to a problem associated with the current sub-task with a question like this:

(5-5)   Should I use the box-end ratchet wrench to do that?

This does not imply a shift to the next sub-task requiring a box-end ratchet wrench (assuming that the current task doesn't require one) (cf Grosz 1977b:105).

We can see here that the problem of the circularity of language comprehension looms dangerously — to determine the focus one must resolve the references, and to resolve the references, one must know the focus. In Grosz's work, the strong constraints of the structure of task-oriented dialogues provide a toehold. Whether generalization to the case of discourse with other structures, or with no particular structure, is possible is unclear, as it may not be possible to determine so nicely what the knowledge associated with any new focus is. (See however my remarks in section 5.1.2 on the relationship between Grosz's work and that of Kantor, and section 5.5 on approaches which attempt to exploit local discourse structure.)

In addition, Grosz's mechanisms are limited in their ability to resolve intersentential and/or inference-requiring anaphora. The assumption that global focus of attention equals all and only possible referents (except where the focus shifts), while perhaps not unreasonable in task-oriented domains, is probably untrue in general. For example, could such mechanisms handle the 'table' examples of Chapter 4, excluding the table from focus when the second sentence of each of these texts is considered? Recall that local as well as global theme is involved (see section 5.1). Similarly, could the level of world knowledge and inference required by the 'sukiyaki' examples of Chapter 3 be integrated into the partitioned semantic net formalism? Could entities evoked by, but not explicit in, a text of only moderate structure be identified and instantiated in focus? Grosz did not address these issues (nor did she need to

5.2.3 Maintaining focus

for her immediate goals), but they would need to be resolved in any attempt to generalize her approach. (Some other related problems, including those of focus shifting, are discussed in Grosz (1978).)

Grosz's contribution was to demonstrate the role of discourse structure in the identification of theme, relevant world knowledge and the resolution of reference; we now turn to another system which aspires to similar goals, but in a more general context.

5.3. Focus in the PAL system and Sidner's theory

The PAL personal assistant program (Bullwinkle 1977a) is a system designed to accept natural language requests for scheduling activities. A typical request (from Bullwinkle 1977b:44) is:

> (5-6) I want to schedule a meeting with Ira. It should be at 3 pm tomor-
> row. We can meet in Bruce's office.

The section of PAL that deals with discourse pragmatics and reference was developed by Candace Sidner [Bullwinkle] (Bullwinkle 1977b; Sidner 1978a). Like Grosz's system (see section 5.2), PAL attempts to find a focus of attention in its knowledge structures to use as a focus for reference resolution. Sidner sees the focus as equivalent to the discourse topic; in fact in Bullwinkle (1977b) the word *topic* is used instead of *focus*.

There are three major differences from Grosz's system:

1 PAL does not rely heavily on discourse structures.

2 Knowledge is represented in frames.

3 Focus selection and shifting are handled at a more superficial level.

I will discuss each difference in turn.

5.3.1. PAL's approach to discourse

Because a request to PAL need not have the rigid structure of one of Grosz's task-oriented dialogues, PAL does not use discourse structure to the same extent, instead relying on more general local cues. However, as we shall see below, in focus selection and shifting, Sidner was forced to use ad hoc rules based on observations of the typical requests to PAL.

5.3.2. The frame as focus

The representation of knowledge in PAL is based on the FRAME concept first introduced by Minsky (1975),[8] and its implementation uses the FRL frame representation language (actually a dialect of LISP) developed by Roberts and Goldstein (1977a, 1977b; Goldstein and Roberts 1977).

In PAL, the frame corresponds to Grosz's focus space. Following Rosenberg's (1976, 1977) work on discourse structure and frames, the antecedent for a definite NP is first assumed to be either the frame itself, or one of its slots.[9] So, for example, in (5-7):

> (5-7) I want to have a meeting with Ross[(1)]. It should be at three pm. The location will be the department lounge. Please tell Ross[(2)].

it refers to the MEETING frame (NOT to the text *a meeting*) which provides the context for the whole discourse; *the location* refers to the LOCATION slot that the MEETING frame presumably has (thus the CLOSELY ASSOCIATED WITH relation (see section 2.4.2) is easily handled), and *Ross*[(2)] to the contents[10] of the CO-MEETER slot, previously given as Ross.

If the antecedent cannot be found in the frame, it is assumed to be either outside the discourse or inferred. In (5-7), PAL would search its database to find referents for *Ross*[(1)] and *the department lounge*. Personal names are resolved with a special module that knows about the semantics of names (Bullwinkle 1977b:48). PAL carries out database searches for references like *the department lounge* apparently by searching a hierarchy of frames, looking at the frames in the slots of the current focus, and then in the slots of these frames, and so on (Sidner 1978a:211) though it is not apparent why this should usefully constrain the search in the above example.[11]

---

[8]I will have to assume the reader is familiar with the basic concept of frames. Readers who require further background should read the section of Charniak (1976) on frames and/or Minsky's original paper (1975).

[9]In Sidner (1978b:91) it is claimed that a definite NP cannot refer to the focus if it contains more information than the focus. This is often true, but (2-100) is a counterexample to the complete generality of her assertion.

[10]Sidner only speaks of reference to slots (1978a:211), without saying whether she means the slot itself or its contents; it seems reasonable to assume, as I have done here, that she actually means both.

[11]In fact there is no need in this particular example for a referent at all. The personal assistant need only treat *the department lounge* as a piece of text, presumably meaningful to both the speaker and Ross, denoting the meeting location. A human might do this when passing on a message they didn't understand:

> (i) Ross asked me to tell you to meet him in the arboretum, whatever the heck that is.

On the other hand, an explicit antecedent WOULD be needed if PAL had been asked, say, to deliver some coffee to the meeting in the department lounge. Knowing when to be satisfied with ignorance is a difficult problem which Sidner does not consider, preferring the safe course of always requiring an antecedent.

5.3.3. Focus selection

In PAL, the initial focus is the first NP following the VP of the first sentence of the discourse — usually, the object of the sentence — or, if there is no such NP, then the subject of that sentence. This is a short-cut method, which seems to be sufficient for requests to PAL, but which Sidner readily admits is inadequate for the general case (Sidner 1978a:209). I will briefly review some of the problems.

Charníak (1978) has shown that the frame-selection problem (which is here identical to the initial focus selection problem, since the focus is just the frame representing the theme of the discourse) is in fact extremely difficult, and is not in the most general case amenable to solution by either strictly top-down or bottom-up methods. Sidner's assumption that the relevant frame is given by an explicitly mentioned NP is also a source of trouble, even in the examples she quotes, such as these two (Sidner 1978b:92):

(5-8) I was driving along <u>the freeway</u> the other day. Suddenly the engine began to make a funny noise.

(5-9) I went to a new <u>restaurant</u> with Sam. The waitress was nasty. The food was great.

(Underlining indicates what Sidner claims is the focus.) In (5-8), Sidner posits a chain of inferences to get from *the engine* to the focus, the FREEWAY frame. This is more complex than is necessary; if the frame/focus were DRIVING (with its LOCATION slot containing the FREEWAY frame), then the path from the frame to *the engine* is shorter and the whole arrangement seems more natural. Thus we see that focus need not be based on an NP at all.

In (5-9), our problem is what to do with Sam, who could be referenced in a subsequent sentence. It is necessary to integrate Sam into the RESTAURANT frame/focus, since clearly he should not be considered external to the discourse and sought in the database. While the RESTAURANT frame may indeed contain a COMPANION slot for Sam to sit in, it is clear that the first sentence could have been *I went <anywhere at all> with Sam*, requiring that any frame referring to something occupying a location have a COMPANION slot. This is clearly undesirable. But the RESTAURANT frame IS involved in (5-9), otherwise *the waitress* and *the food* would be external to the discourse. A natural solution is that the frame/focus of (5-9) is actually the GOING-SOMEWHERE frame (with Sam in its COMPANION slot), containing the RESTAURANT frame in its PLACE slot, with both frames together taken as the focus. Sidner does not consider mechanisms for a multi-frame focus.

It is, of course, not always true that the frame/focus is explicit. Charniak (1978) points out that (5-10) is somehow sufficient to invoke the MAGICIAN frame:

(5-10) The woman waved as the man on stage sawed her in half.

(See also Hirst (1982) for more on frame invocation problems.)

Focus shifting in PAL is restricted: the only shifts permitted are to and from sub-aspects of the present focus (Sidner 1978a:209). Old topics are stacked for possible later return. This is very similar to Grosz's open-focus hierarchy. It is unclear whether there is a predictive aspect to PAL's focus-shift mechanism,[12] but the basic idea seems to be that any new phrase in a sentence is picked as a potential new focus. If in a subsequent sentence an anaphoric reference is a semantically acceptable coreferent for that potential focus, then a shift to that focus is ipso facto indicated (Sidner 1978a:209). Presumably this check is done after a check of focus has failed, but before any database search. A potential focus has a limited life span, and is dropped if not shifted to by the end of the second sentence following the one in which it occurred.

An example (Sidner 1978a:209):

(5-11) I want to schedule a meeting with George, Jim, Steve and Mike. We can meet in my office. {It's kind of small, but the meeting won't last long anyway | It won't take more than 20 minutes}.

In the second sentence *my office* is identified as a potential focus, and *it*, in the first reading of the third sentence, as an acceptable coreferent to *my office* confirms the shift. In the second reading, *it* couldn't be *my office*, so no shift occurs. The acceptability decision is based on selectional and case-like restrictions.

While perhaps adequate for PAL, this mechanism is, of course, not sufficient for the general case, where a true shift, as opposed to an expansion upon a previously mentioned point, may occur. This is exemplified by many of the shifts in Grosz's task-oriented dialogues.

Another problem arising from this shift mechanism is that two different focus shifts may be indicated at the same time, but the mechanism has no way to choose between them. For example:

(5-12) Schedule a meeting of the Experimental Theology Research Group, and tell Ross Andrews about it too. I'd like him to hear about the deocommunication work that they're doing.

Each of the underlined NPs in the first sentence would be picked as a potential focus. Since each is pronominally referenced in the second sentence, the mechanism would be confused as to where to shift the focus. (Presumably *Ross Andrews* would be the correct choice here.)

---

[12] On page 209 of Sidner (1978a) we are told: "Focus shifts cannot be predicted; they are detectable only after they occur". Yet on the following page, Sidner says: "Sentences appearing in mid-discourse are assumed to be about the focus until the coreference module predicts a focus shift...Once an implicit focus relation is established, the module can go onto [sic] predictions of focus shift". My interpretation of these remarks is that one cannot be certain that the next sentence will shift focus, but one CAN note when a shift MIGHT happen, requiring later checking to confirm or disconfirm the shift.

5.3.3 Focus selection

I always get buggered by the
bottom-up approach.
   — *"Sydney J Hurtubise"*[13]

5.3.4. Sidner's general theory

In another paper (Sidner 1978b) Sidner describes a more general theory of focus whose relation to PAL is not explicitly stated. For example, for details of focus shifting one is simply referred to the section of Bullwinkle (1977b) on PAL's shift mechanism, which, as we saw, is inadequate for the general case. One can't tell if Sidner intends that PAL's mechanism be part of her general theory, or merely makes the reference as a stopgap.

Her theory is based on Grosz's system, but does not rely on a rigid discourse structure, nor does it suggest a knowledge representation for focus. However, Sidner does suggest (1978b:92) that a semantic association network should be involved as well. This would be used in determining CLOSELY ASSOCI-ATED WITH relations (Sidner 1978b:92), though she doesn't say how an accept-able closeness would be determined in the net. The net would be used instead of, or together with, the database search, the search starting from concepts closely related to the focus and working outwards. When a reference's relation-ship to the focus requires inference, this too would use the semantic net, though we are not told if this is attempted before, after, in parallel with or as part of the database search, nor exactly how it would be done.

Sidner is also concerned, in her general theory, with deciding whether or not a definite NP is generic. (Grosz did not attempt this, assuming all refer-ences to be specific.)[14] Sidner gives some heuristics for determining whether a U-AMBIGUOUS NP — one that could be either generic or non-generic — has a pre-ferred generic or non-generic reading. She then points out that those NPs whose head nouns match the focus usually have the same genericity as the focus, with which they are coreferential. She gives these examples (1978b:91):

---

[13]While presenting a paper at the first national conference of the Canadian Society for Compu-tational Studies of Intelligence/Societe canadienne pour etudes d'intelligence par ordinateur, on 26 August 1976.

[14]A SPECIFIC NP refers to a certain entity, a GENERIC NP to a class of entity, but via a single member of the class. For example, (i) shows specific NPs and (ii) a generic NP:

   (i) When <u>Ross</u> returned to <u>his car</u>, <u>the wheels</u> were gone.

   (ii) Today we will discuss rare marsupials. First let me tell you about <u>the narbalek</u>.

Note that the second sentence of (ii) has a generic reading in this context, but can be specific in a different context:

   (iii)Ross gave Nadia a narbalek and a bandicoot. First let me tell you about <u>the narbalek</u>.

An NP may be ATTRIBUTIVE instead of either specific or generic — this usage need not concern us here.

(5-13) I'm going to tell you about the elephant[1]. The elephant[2] is the largest of the jungle mammals. He weighs over 3000 pounds.

(5-14) I sent George an elephant[3] last year for a birthday present. The elephant[4] likes potatoes for breakfast.

The underlined NPs are u-ambiguous without context. But since the focus of (5-13), *the elephant*[1], is generic, so are *the elephant*[2] and *he*; the focus of (5-14), *an elephant*[3], is specific, and therefore so is *the elephant*[4]. The focus can thus be used to u-disambiguate such NPs. Unfortunately there are counterexamples to this; Sidner's is (5-15):

(5-15) Mary got a ferret[1] for Christmas last year. The ferret[2] is a very rare animal.

The ferret[2] is so strongly generic that the specific focus, Mary's ferret, cannot override it, and *the ferret*[2] therefore does not refer to the focus. Hence genericity must also be checked at the sentence level before testing NPs to see if they refer to the focus. In other words, there is a top-down/bottom-up conflict here. Sidner's solution is apparently to first check whether an NP is overwhelmingly generic at the sentence level; if not, only then is the genericity of the focus used. No threshold for overwhelming genericity is suggested.

Sidner's general theory has a more complex initial focus selection mechanism than PAL; she refers the reader to her forthcoming thesis (Sidner 1979) for details.

5.3.5. Conclusions

The shortcomings of Sidner's work are mainly attributable to two causes: her avoidance of relying on the highly constrained discourse structures that Grosz used, and the limited connectivity of frame systems, compared to Grosz's semantic nets. Recognizing the latter point, Sidner proposed the use of an association network in her general theory (1978b:87), though she does not say whether this should supplant or supplement other knowledge structures like PAL's frames. (Perhaps a synthesis, such as a network whose nodes are frames (cf McCalla 1977), is the answer.) With respect to the former point, perhaps Sidner's main contribution has been to show the difficulties and pitfalls that lie in wait for anyone attempting to generalize Grosz's work, even to the extent that PAL does.

5.4. Webber's formalism

In the preceding sections of this chapter, we saw approaches to focus that were mainly top-down in that they relied on a notion of theme and/or focus of attention to guide the selection of focus (although theme determination may have been bottom-up). An alternative approach has been suggested by Bonnie Lynn [Nash-]Webber (Nash-Webber and Reiter 1977; Webber 1978a, 1978b), wherein a set of rules is applied to a logical-form representation of the text to derive the set of entities that that text makes available for subsequent reference. Webber's formalism attacks problems caused by quantification, such as those we saw in (2-5)[15] that have not otherwise been considered by workers in NLU.

I can only give the flavour of Webber's formalism here, and I shall have to assume some familiarity with logical forms. Readers who want more details should see her thesis (1978a); readers who find my exposition mystifying should not worry unduly − the fault is probably mine − but turn to the thesis for illumination.

In Webber's formalism, it is assumed that an input sentence is first converted to a parse tree, and then, by some semantic interpretation process, to an EXTENDED RESTRICTED-QUANTIFICATION PREDICATE CALCULUS REPRESENTATION. It is during this second conversion that anaphor resolution takes place. When the final representation, which we shall simply call a LOGICAL FORM, is complete, certain rules are applied to it to generate the set of referable entities and descriptions that the sentence evokes. Webber considers three types of antecedents − those for definite pronouns (IRAs), those for *one*-anaphora, and those for verb phrase ellipsis. Each has its own set of rules, at which we will briefly look.

5.4.1. Definite pronouns

The antecedents for definite pronouns are INVOKING DESCRIPTIONS (IDs), which are derived from the logical form representation of a sentence by a set of rules that attempt to take into account factors, such as NP definiteness or references to sets, that affect what antecedents are evoked by a text. There are six of these ID-rules;[16] which one applies depends on the structural description of the logical form.

Here is one of Webber's examples (1978a:64):

(5-16) Wendy bought a crayon.

This has this representation:

---

[15](2-5) Ross gave each girl a crayon. <u>They</u> used <u>them</u> to draw pictures of Daryel in the bath.

[16]Webber regards her rules only as a preliminary step towards a complete set which considers all relevant factors. She discusses some of the remaining problems, such as negation, in Webber (1978a:81-88).

(5-17) $(\exists x : \text{Crayon})$. Bought Wendy,x

Now, one of the ID-rules says that any sentence S whose representation is of this form:

(5-18) $(\exists x : C)$. Fx

where C is an arbitrary predicate on individuals and Fx an arbitrary open sentence in which x is free, evokes an entity whose representation is of this form:

(5-19) e_j ιx: Cx & Fx & evoke S,x

where e_j is an arbitrary label assigned to the entity and ι is the definite operator. Hence, starting at the left of (5-17), we obtain this representation for the crayon of (5-16):

(5-20) e_1 ιx: Crayon x & Bought Wendy,x & evoke (5-16),x

which may be interpreted as "e_1 is the crayon mentioned in sentence (5-16) that Wendy bought". Similarly we will obtain a representation of e_2, Wendy, which is then substituted for *Wendy* in (5-20) after some matching process has determined their identity.

In this next, more complex, example, (Webber 1978a:73) we see how quantification is handled:

(5-21) Each boy gave each girl a peach.
$\quad\quad$ $(\forall x : \text{Boy})$ $(\forall y : \text{Girl})$ $(\exists z : \text{Peach})$. Gave x,y,z

This matches the following structural description (where Q_j stands for the quantifier $(\forall x_j \in e_j)$, where e_j is an earlier evoked discourse entity, and ! is the left boundary of a clause):

(5-22) $!Q_1 \cdots Q_n$ $(\exists y : C)$. Fy

and hence evokes an ID of this form:

(5-23) e_i ιy :$maxset(\lambda(u : C)[(\exists x_1 \in e_1) \cdots (\exists x_n \in e_n)$. Fu
$\quad\quad$ & evokeS,u]) y

(For any predicate X, $maxset(X)$ is a predicate true if and only if its argument is the maximal set of all items for which X is true. λ is the abstraction operator.) Another rule has already given us:

(5-24) e_1 ιx : $maxset(\text{Boy})x$ $\quad\quad$ e_2 ιx : $maxset(\text{Girl})x$
$\quad\quad$ "the set of all boys" $\quad\quad\quad\quad$ "the set of all girls"

and so (5-23) is instantiated as:

5.4.1 *Definite pronouns*

(5-25) e_3 iz $:maxset$ $(\lambda(u : Peach)[(\exists x \in e_1)(\exists y \in e_2)$. Gave x,y,u
      & evoke (5-21),y]) z
      "the set of peaches, each one of which is linked to (5-21) by vir-
tue of some member of e_1 giving it to some member of e_2.

Although such rules could (in principle) be used to generate all IDs (focus
elements) that a sentence evokes, Webber does not commit herself to such an
approach, instead allowing for the possibility of generating IDs only when they
are needed, depending on subsequent information such as speaker's perspec-
tive. She also suggests the possibility of "vague, temporary" IDs for interim use
(1978a:67).

There is a problem here with intrasentential anaphora, since it is assumed
that a sentence's anaphors are resolved before ID rules are applied to find what
may be the antecedents necessary for that resolution. Webber proposes that
known syntactic and selectional constraints may help in this conflict, but this is
not always sufficient. For example:

(5-26) Mary bought each girl a cotton T-shirt, but none of <u>them</u> were the
       style de rigeur in high schools.

The IDs for both the set of girls and the set of T-shirts are needed to resolve
them, but *them* needs to be resolved before the IDs are generated. In this particular example, the clear solution is to work a clause at a time rather than at a
sentence level. However, this is not always an adequate solution, as (5-27)
shows:

(5-27) The rebel students annoyed the teachers greatly, and by the end of
       the week none of the faculty were willing to go to <u>their</u> classes.

In this ambiguous sentence one possible antecedent for *their, the faculty*,
occurs in the same clause as the anaphor. Thus neither strictly intraclausal
nor strictly interclausal methods are appropriate. Webber is aware of this
problem (1978a:48), and believes that it suffices that such information as is
available be used to rule out impossible choices; the use of vague temporary
IDs then allows the anaphor to be resolved.

5.4.2. *One*-anaphors

The second type of anaphor Webber discusses is the *ONE*-ANAPHOR.[17] By this, she
means an anaphor that refers to a description rather than a specific entity (see
section 2.5). For example (Webber 1978a:97):

---

[17]I feel *one-anaphor* is a misleading (as well as clumsy) term, since a *one*-anaphor can be instantiated by *that, those, it,* or ϕ as well as *one*. Perhaps Webber's earlier term *descriptional
anaphor* (Nash-Webber 1976) would have been better.

(5-28) Wendy didn't give either boy a green tie-dyed T-shirt, but she gave Sue a red <u>one</u>.

Here *one* is either *T-shirt* or *tie-dyed T-shirt*, but not *green tie-dyed T-shirt*.

Webber believes that the logical-form representation, as used above for deriving IDs, is an adequate representation from which such descriptions may be derived when needed by an appropriate reasoning procedure. She argues that this representation fulfils four desiderata:

1 It must retain the structure of noun phrases as a unit (so that, for example, in (5-28) *tie-dyed* remains connected to *T-shirt* to provide a single antecedent).

2 Yet it must allow decomposition of the description (so that, for example, in (5-28) *green* can be broken off *green tie-dyed T-shirt* when found inappropriate).

3 It should allow identification of word sense, to prevent inadvertent syllepsoid/zeugmoid interpretations (so that, for example, (5-29):

(5-29) *The ruler [i.e. head of state] picked <u>one</u> [i.e. a ruler, i.e. a measuring stick] up and measured the lamp.

can be flagged as anomalous).[18]

4 It must retain definite pronouns in both their resolved and unresolved forms (so that, for example, in (5-30) (after Webber 1978a:106):

(5-30) I compared Ross's behaviourist analysis of <u>his</u> mother with Daryel's gestalt <u>one</u>.

one is resolved as *analysis of Ross's mother*, not *analysis of Daryel's mother*, while in (5-31) (after Webber 1978a:106):

(5-31) Sue will pay up to seventy dollars for a dress <u>she</u> can wear without alteration, but Nadia refuses to pay more than fifty for <u>one</u>.

one is a dress that Nadia, not Sue, can wear without alteration).

Given this approach, the problem remains of determining when an anaphor is a *one*-anaphor and when it is a definite anaphor, as some pronouns, such as *it*, can be either. Webber offers some tentative suggestions:

1 *That* and *those* are *one*-anaphors if and only if they are followed by one or more NP postmodifiers (such as a prepositional phrase or relative clause).

2 An ellipsis can be used as a *one*-anaphor when preceded by an adjective but not followed by a postmodifer, or when preceded by a possessive, ordinal, comparative or superlative (with optional postmodifier). However, the problem of detecting the ellipsis in the first place remains, as structural

---

[18]See footnote 32 of Chapter 2.

5.4.2 One-anaphors

ambiguities can arise (Webber 1978a:116).

3 *It* is problematic, but it seems to be a *one*-anaphor whenever followed by a postmodifier, and it requires as an antecedent a description of a unique entity in the discourse.

Webber asserts (1978a:111) that only recency, independent of discourse structure, controls the availability of descriptions as antecedents. I'm not sure that this is entirely correct. For example:

(5-32) ?Ross drank the wine on the table. Meanwhile Nadia and Sue played cards on another <u>one</u> next door.

(5-33) ?Ross moved the wine on the table to another <u>one</u>.

In each of these texts an attempt to reference a recent description with *one* is ill-formed, or at best marginal. That is, not all recent descriptions are in focus. Are, conversely, all referable descriptions textually recent? The answer is probably yes; I for one have not found any counterexamples.

Only descriptions explicitly present in the text are available as antecedents in the approach mentioned so far. What of implicit descriptions evoked by the text, which are also referable? Webber divides these into three categories, and gives suggestions on the handling of each (1978a:118-124):

1 Strained anaphora (see section 2.3.5). Webber suggests strained anaphora can occur with only a certain few words, and therefore can be handled by noting all such cases in the lexicon. I find this intellectually unsatisfying — I'm sure there is a general principle lurking about waiting to be discovered — but I have no better suggestions to offer.

2 References to IDs evoked by existential quantifiers. For example (after Webber 1978a:120):

(5-34) Nadia gave Ross some cotton T-shirts. The most expensive ϕ was too large, but the other <u>ones</u> fitted.

The referents in (5-34) are not just *cotton T-shirt(s)* but *cotton T-shirt(s) that Nadia gave Ross*. Two ways of deriving these are suggested: either *(a)* the *one*-anaphors could be treated as above, referring only to *cotton T-shirt(s)*, and these references are in turn treated as again anaphoric (cf section 2.4.2) and resolved as definite references to the ID for the T-shirts that Nadia gave Ross; or *(b)* the *one*-anaphors may be viewed as direct references to the ID. The latter has problems with negation[19] and blurs the useful line between *one*- and definite anaphors; the former requires great care with determiners when checking whether a resolved *one*-anaphor has turned into a definite anaphor.

3 Abstraction of list elements. For example (Webber 1978a:122-123):

---

[19]*One*-anaphors can refer to descriptions of entities that don't exist in the discourse model and therefore don't have IDs. See Webber (1978a:121).

(5-35) I have in my cellar a '76 Beaujolais, a '71 Chateau Figeac, a '75 Durkheimer Feuerburg and a '75 Ockfener Bockstein. Shall we drink the German <u>ones</u> now and the others later?

(5-36) I know about Advent, Bose, AR and KLH, but about Japanese <u>ones</u> you'll have to ask Fred.

According to Webber, *ones* is *wines* in (5-35) and something like *speakers* or *speaker manufacturers* in (5-36). This sort of sentence varies in acceptability (I personally find (5-36) ill-formed) and Webber suggests that the poorer sentences are exactly those where the anaphor occurs in an indefinite NP, requiring an explicit abstraction on the list to be carried out for use as an antecedent, whereas in sentences such as (5-35) *one(s)* can be interpreted simply as *member(s) of the just-mentioned list.*[20]

5.4.3. Verb phrase ellipsis

The third and last class of anaphor that Webber treats is verb phrase ellipsis (VPE) (in which she includes the pro-verb *to do*),[21] extending Sag's (1976) theory of logical forms and VPE. A verb phrase may be elided if its logical form representation (written such that the predicate of the sentence applies to the subject) is identical to that of some preceding[22] VP, called the ellipsis TRIGGER. (The ANTECEDENT is the deleted VP itself.) For example:

(5-37) Ross gave Nadia a book. Sue <u>did</u> ϕ too.
$\lambda(s)$[Gave, s, Nadia, book] Ross
$\lambda(s)$[Gave, s, Nadia, book] Sue

Webber proposes that a syntactic variant of her abovementioned representation is adequate for resolving VPE, discussing (1978a:129-149) the requirements that it must and does fulfil, including the problems caused by negation

---

[20]In my idiolect such a sentence is ill-formed exactly when this simpler interpretation of *one(s)* is not possible. Webber believes that the additional requirement that the list be composed of names, not descriptions, is necessary, and thus does not like this example of hers (1978a:124):

(i) At the Paris zoo, Bruce saw a lion, a tiger, a giraffe, a hippopotamus and an elephant. It was feeding time, and the carnivorous <u>ones</u> were eating boeuf bourgignon, and the herbivorous <u>ones</u>, salad niçoise.

However, this is acceptable to me, and is amenable to the simpler interpretation. On the other hand, the list of animals in (i) is, in a very real sense, a list of names rather than descriptions. (Where is the dividing line between a name and a description?) It may therefore be that Webber's explanation is correct and that she has misconstrued her own example.

[21]Webber sees *to do* as a dummy verb sitting in the void left by a VPE, rather than as an anaphor in its own right.

[22]Cataphoric VPE is also possible, but heavily restricted. Webber discusses it briefly (1978a:152).

and sloppy identity (see section 2.6).

The focus for VPE is then the set of all possible triggers in the logical form representation. Recency, with the additional constraints of sentence structure, voice, negation and tense, determines what is available as a trigger. When an ellipsis is detected, the appropriate trigger is sought; Webber discusses this and associated problems in (1978a:157-162). In particular, it is necessary to resolve VPE before definite pronouns, to avoid problems of missing antecedents (see footnote 59 of Chapter 2).

As Webber herself points out, this approach only works where the trigger is textually similar to the elided VP. But this is not always the case. Recall texts (2-16) and (2-17),[23] for example. This type of VPE requires inference and/or alternative ways of looking at the text; Webber makes some very tentative suggestions on how this might be handled (1978a:162-167).

5.4.4. Conclusions

It remains to discuss the strengths and weaknesses of Webber's approach, and she herself (in contradistinction to some other AI workers) is as quick to point out the latter as the former. The reader is therefore referred to her thesis (1978a) for this. However, I will make some global comments on the important aspects relevant here.

Webber's main contributions, as I see them, are as follows:

1 The focus problem is approached from the point of view of determining what an adequate representation would be, rather that trying to fit (to straitjacket?) focus into some pre-existing and perhaps arbitrarily chosen representation; and the criteria of adequacy for the representation are rigorously enumerated.

2 A formalism in which it is possible to compute focus elements as they are needed, rather than having them sitting round in advance (as in Grosz's (1977) system), perhaps never to be used, is provided (but compare my further remarks below).

3 Webber brings to NLU anaphora research the formality and rigour of logic, something that has been previously almost unseen.

4 Previously ignored problems of quantification are dealt with.

5 The formalism itself is an important contribution.

The shortcomings, as I see them, are as follows:

1 The formalism relies very much on antecedents being in the text. Entities evoked by, but not explicit in, the text cannot in general be adequately handled (contrary to Grosz's system).

---

[23](2-16) Nadia wants to climb Mt Everest, and Ross wants to tour Africa, but neither of them will ϕ because they are both too poor.
(2-17) Ross and Nadia wanted to dance together, but Nadia's mother said she couldn't ϕ.

2 The formalism is not related to discourse structure. So, for example, it contains nothing to discourage the use of *the table* as the antecedent in the 'table' examples of Chapter 4. It remains to be seen if discourse pragmatics can be adequately integrated with the formalism or otherwise accounted for in a system using the formalism.

3 Intrasentential and intraclausal anaphora are not adequately dealt with.

4 Webber does not relate her discussions of representational adequacy to currently popular knowledge representations. If frames, for example, are truly inadequate we would like to have some watertight proof of this before abandoning current NLU projects attempting to use frames.

You will have noticed that contribution 2 and shortcoming 1 are actually two sides of the same coin — it is static pre-available knowledge that allows non-textual entities to be easily found — and clearly a synthesis will be necessary here.

5.5. Discourse-cohesion approaches to anaphora resolution

Another approach to coreference resolution attempts to exploit local discourse cohesion, building a representation of the discourse with which references can be resolved. This approach has been taken by (inter alia) Klappholz and Lockman (again hereafter *K&L*) (1977; Lockman 1978). By using only cues to the discourse structure at the sentence level or lower, one avoids the need to search for referents in pre-determined dialogue models such as those of Grosz's task-oriented dialogues (see section 5.2), or rigidly predefined knowledge structures such as scripts (Schank and Abelson 1975, 1977) and frames (Minsky 1975), which K&L, for example, see as overweight structures that inflexibly dominate processing of text. K&L emphasize that the structure through which reference is resolved must be dynamically built up as the text is processed; frames or scripts could assist in this building, but cannot, however, be reliably used for reference resolution as deviations by the text from the pre-defined structure will cause errors.

The basis of this approach is that there is a strong interrelationship between coreference and the cohesive ties in a discourse that make it coherent. By determining what the cohesive ties in a discourse are, one can put each new sentence or clause, as it comes in, into the appropriate place in a growing structure that represents the discourse. This structure can then be used as a focus to search for coreference antecedents, since not only do coherently connected sentences tend to refer to the same things, but knowledge of the cohesion relation can provide additional reference resolution restraints. Hobbs (1978) in particular sees the problem of coreference resolution as being automatically solved in the process of discovering the coherence relations in a text. (An example of this will be given in section 5.5.2.) Conversely, it is frequently helpful or necessary to resolve coreference relations in order to discover the coherence relations. This is not a vicious circle, claims

Hobbs, but a spiral staircase. (This helical approach to understanding also occurs elsewhere in artificial intelligence; compare for example Mackworth's (1978) Cycle of Perception.)

In our discussion below, we will cover four issues:

1 deciding on a set of possible coherence relations;

2 detecting them when they occur in a text;

3 using the coherence relations to build a focus structure; and

4 searching for referents in the structure.

5.5.1. Coherence relations

The first thing required by this approach is a complete and computable set of the coherence relations that may obtain between sentences and/or clauses. Various sets have been suggested by many people, including Eisenstadt (1976), Phillips (1977), Pitkin (1977a, 1977b), Hirst (1977b, 1978b), Lockman (1978), Hobbs (1978) and Reichman (1978a, 1978b).[24] None of these sets fulfil all desiderata; and while Halliday and Hasan (1976) provide an extensive analysis of cohesion, it does not fit within our computational framework of coherence relations, and those, such as Hobbs, Lockman, Eisenstadt and Hirst, who emphasize computability, provide small sets which cannot, I believe, capture all the semantic subtleties of discourse cohesion. Nevertheless, the works cited above undoubtedly serve as a useful starting point for development of this area.

To illustrate what a very preliminary set of cohesion relations could look like, I will briefly present a set abstracted from the various sets of Eisenstadt, Hirst, Hobbs, Lockman and Phillips (but not faithful to any one of these).

The set contains two basic classes of coherence relations: *(a)* expansion or elaboration on an entity, concept or event in the discourse, and *(b)*temporal continuation or time flow. Expansion includes relations like CONTRAST, CAUSE, EFFECT, SYLLOGISM, ELABORATION, PARALLEL and EXEMPLIFICATION. In the following examples, "▪" is used to indicate the point where the cohesive tie illustrated is acting:

(5-38) [CONTRAST] The hoary marmot likes to be scratched behind the ears by its mate, ▪ while in the lesser dormouse, nuzzling is the primary behaviour promoting pair-bonding.

(5-39) [CAUSE] Ross scratched his head furiously. ▪ The new Hoary Marmot™ shampoo that he used had made it itch unbearably.

(5-40) [EFFECT] Ross pulled out the bottom module. ▪ The entire structure collapsed.

---

[24]Reichman's coherence relations operate at paragraph level rather than sentence or clause level.

(5-41) [SYLLOGISM] Nadia goes to the movies with Ross on Fridays. Today's Friday, ▪ so I guess she'll be going to the movies.

(5-42) [ELABORATION] To gain access to the latch-housing, remove the control panel cover. ▪ Undo both screws and rock it gently until it snaps out from the mounting bracket.

(5-43) [PARALLEL] Nearly all our best men are dead! Carlyle, Tennyson, Browning, George Eliot! − ▪ I'm not feeling very well myself![25]

(5-44) [EXEMPLIFICATION] Many of our staff are keen amateur ornithologists. ▪ Nadia has written a book on the Canadian triller, and Daryel once missed a board meeting because he was high up a tree near Gundaroo, watching the hatching of some rare red-crested snipes.

(You may disagree with my classification of some of the relations above; the boundaries between categories are yet ill-defined, and it is to be expected that some people will find that their intuitive boundaries differ from mine.)

Temporal flow relations involve some continuation forwards or backwards over time:

(5-45) VICTORIA − A suntanned Prince Charles arrived here Sunday afternoon, ▪ and was greeted with a big kiss by a pretty English au pair girl.[26]

(5-46) SAN JUAN, Puerto Rico − Travel officials tackled a major job here Sunday to find new accommodations for 650 passengers from the burned Italian cruise liner *Angelina Lauro*.
▪ The vessel caught fire Friday while docked at Charlotte Amalie in the Virgin Islands, but most passengers were ashore at the time.[27]

Temporal flow may be treated as a single relation, as Phillips, for example, does, or it may be subdivided, as Eisenstadt and Hirst do, into categories like TIME STEP, FLASHBACK, FLASHFORWARD, TIME EDIT, and so on. Certainly, time flow in a text may be quite contorted, as in (5-47) (from Hirst 1978b); "▪" indicates a point where the direction of the time flow changes:

(5-47) Slowly, hesitantly, Ross approached Nadia. ▪ He had waited for this moment for many days. ▪ Now he was going to say the words ▪ which he had agonized over ▪ and in the very room ▪ he had often dreamed about. ▪ He gazed lovingly at her soft green eyes.

It is not clear, however, to what extent an analysis of time flow is necessary for anaphor resolution. I suspect that relatively little is necessary − less than is required for other aspects of discourse understanding. Temporal anaphora

---

[25] From: A lament [cartoon caption]. *Punch, or the London charivari*, CIC, 1893, page 210.

[26] From: *The Vancouver express*, 2 April 1979, page A1.

[27] From: *The Vancouver express*, 2 April 1979, page A5.

5.5.1 Coherence relations

(see section 5.6.1) probably makes the strongest demands here, though the definitive set of temporal cohesion relations will probably be a superset of those actually required to resolve anaphors.

I see relations like those exemplified above as PRIMITIVES from which more complex relations could be built. For example, the relation between the two sentences of (5-40) above clearly involves FORWARD TIME STEP as well as EFFECT. I have hypothesized elsewhere (Hirst 1978b) the possibility of constructing a small set of discourse relations (with cardinality about twenty or less) from which more complex relations may be built up by simple combination, and, one hopes, in such a way that the effects of relation $R1+R2$ would be the sum of the individual effects of relations $R1$ and $R2$. Rules for permitted combinations would be needed; for example, FORWARD TIME STEP could combine with EFFECT, but not with BACKWARD TIME STEP.

What would the formal definition of a coherence relation be like? Here is Hobbs's (1978:11) definition of ELABORATION: Sentence $S1$ is an ELABORATION of sentence $S0$ if a proposition P follows from the assertions of both $S0$ and $S1$, but $S1$ contains a property of one of the elements of P that is not in $S0$.

5.5.2. An example of anaphor resolution using a coherence relation

It is appropriate at this stage to give an example of the use of coherence relations in the resolution of anaphors. I will present an outline of one of Hobbs's; for the fine details I have omitted, see Hobbs (1978:18-23). The text is this:

(5-48) John can open Bill's safe. He knows the combination.

We want an NLU system to recognize the cohesion relation operating here, namely ELABORATION, and identify *he* as John and *the combination* as that of Bill's safe. We assume that in the world knowledge the system has are various axioms and rules of inference dealing with such matters as what combinations of safes are and knowledge about doing things. Then, from the first sentence of (5-48), which we represent as (5-49):

(5-49) can (John, open (Bill's-safe))

(we omit the details of the representation of *Bill's safe*), we can infer:

(5-50) know (John, cause (do (John, *ACT*), open (Bill's-safe)))
        "John knows an action *ACT* that he can do that will bring about the state in which Bill's-safe is open"

From the second sentence of (5-48), namely:

(5-51) know (HE, combination ($COMB$, Y))
     "someone, HE, knows the combination $COMB$ to something, Y"

we can infer, using knowledge about combinations:

(5-52) know (HE, cause (dial ($COMB$, Y), open (Y)))
     "HE knows that by causing the dialling of $COMB$ on Y, the state
in which Y is open will be brought about"

Recognizing that (5-50) and (5-52) are nearly identical, and assuming that some
coherence relation does hold, we can identify HE with John, Y with Bill's-safe,
and the definition of the ELABORATION relation is satisfied. In the process, the
required referents were found.

5.5.3. Lockman's contextual reference resolution algorithm

Given a set of discourse cohesion relations, how may they be computationally
determined in the processing of a text and used to build a structure representing the discourse that can be used for reference resolution? Only Hobbs (1978)
and Lockman (1978; Klappholz and Lockman 1977) seem to have considered
these aspects of the problem, though Eisenstadt (1976) discusses some of the
requirements in world knowledge and inference that would be required. In this
section we look at Lockman's work; a full description of Hobbs's program was
not available at the time of writing.

Lockman does not separate the three processes of recognizing cohesion,
resolving references and building the representation of the discourse. Rather,
as befits such interrelated processes, all three are carried out at the same
time. His contextual reference resolution algorithm (CRRA) works as follows:

The structure to be built is a tree, initially null, each node of which is a
sentence.   As each new sentence comes in, the CRRA tries to find the right
node of the tree to attach it to, starting at the leaf that is the previous sentence and working back up the tree in a specified search order (see below) until
a connection is indicated. Lockman assumes the existence of a judgement
mechanism which generates and tests hypotheses as to how the new sentence
may be FEASIBLY CONNECTED to the node being tested. The first hypothesis whose
likelihood exceeds a certain threshold is chosen.

The hypotheses consider both the coherence and the coreference relations
that may obtain. Each member of the set of coherence relations is
hypothesized, and for each one coreference relations between the conceptual
tokens of the new sentence and tokens either in the node under consideration
or nearby it in the tree. (The search for tokens goes back as far as necessary
in the tree until suitable ones are found for all unfulfilled definite noun
phrases.) The hypotheses are considered in parallel; if none are judged
sufficiently likely, the next node or set of nodes will be considered for feasible

connection to the current sentence.

The search order is as follows: First the IMMEDIATE CONTEXT, the previous sentence, is tried. If no feasible connection is found, then the immediate ancestor of this node, and all its other descendents, are tried in parallel. If the algorithm is still unsuccessful, the immediate ancestor of the immediate ancestor, and the descendents thereof, are tried, and so on up the tree. If a test of several nodes in parallel yields mode than one acceptable node, the one nearest the immediate context is chosen.

If the current sentence is not a simple sentence, it is not broken into clauses dealt with individually, but rather converted to a small sub-tree, reflecting the semantic relationship between the clauses. The conversion is based simply upon the structure of the parse tree of the sentence and uses a table look-up. One of the nodes is designated by the table look-up as the head node, and the sub-tree is attached to the pre-existing context, using the procedure described above, with the connection occurring at this node. Similarly one (or more) of the nodes is designated as the immediate context, the starting point for the next search. (The search will be conducted in parallel if there is more than one immediate context node.)

There are some possible problems with Lockman's approach. The first lies in the fact that the structure built grows without limit, and therefore searches in it could, in theory, run right through an enormous tree. Normally, of course, a feasible connection or desired referent will be found fairly quickly, close to the immediate context. However, should the judgement mechanism fail to spot the correct one, the algorithm may run wild, searching large areas of the structure needlessly and expensively, possibly lighting on a wrong referent or wrong node for attachment, with no indication that an error has occurred. In other words, Lockman's CRRA places much greater trust in the judgement mechanism than a system like Grosz's (1977) (see section 5.2) which constrains the referent search area — more trust than perhaps should be put in what will of needs be the most tentative and unreliable part of the system.

Secondly, I am worried about the syntax-based table look-up for sub-trees for complex sentences. On the one hand, it would be nice if it were correct, simplifying processing. On the other hand, I cannot but feel that it is an oversimplification, and that effects of discourse theme cannot reliably be handled like this. However, I have no counterexamples to give, and suggest that this question needs more investigation.

The third possible problem, and perhaps the most serious, concerns the order in which the search for a feasible connection takes place. Because the first hypothesis exceeding the likelihood threshold is selected, it is possible to miss an even better hypothesis further up the tree. In theory, this could be avoided by doing all tests in parallel, the winning hypothesis being judged on both likelihood and closeness to the immediate context. In practice, given the ever-growing context tree as discussed above, this would not be feasible, and some way to limit the search area would be needed.

The fourth problem lies in the judgement mechanism itself. Lockman frankly admits that the mechanism, incorporated as a black box in his algorithm, must have abilities far beyond those of present state-of-the-art

5.5.3 Lockman's contextual reference resolution algorithm

inference and judgement systems. The problem is that it is unwise to predicate too much on the nature of this unbuilt black box, as we do not know yet if its input-output behaviour could be as Lockman posits. It may well be that to perform as required, the mechanism will need access to information such as the sentence following the current one (in effect, the ability to delay a decision), or more information about the previous context than the CRRA retains or ever determines; in fact, it may need an entirely different discourse structure representation from the tree being built. In other words, while it is fine in theory to design a reference resolver round a black box, in practice it may be computationally more economical to design the reference resolver round a knowledge of how the black box actually works, exploiting that mechanism, rather than straitjacketing the judgement module into its pre-defined cabinet; thus Lockman's work may be premature.

None of these problems are insurmountable. However it is perhaps a little unfortunate that Lockman's work offers little of immediate use for NLU systems of the present day.

5.5.4. Conclusion

Clearly, much work remains to be done if the coherence/cohesion paradigm of NLU is to be viable. Almost all aspects need refinement. However, it is an intuitively appealling paradigm, and it will be interesting to see if it can be developed into functioning NLU systems.

5.6. Non-noun-phrase focusing

The theories and approaches discussed heretofore in this chapter have been almost exclusively concerned with anaphors whose antecedents are NPs or other noun-like entities in consciousness, and indeed this is where most of the interesting problems lie. However, as we saw in Chapter 2, there are many other kinds of anaphor, and in this section I would like to describe the focus that temporal and locative anaphors require. These are simpler than the nominal case, and I present what I believe to be a complete theory (i.e. one which accounts for all cases).[28]

---

[28]A note on methodology:

In what I say below, I will make assertions like the following:

(i) Linguistic phenomenon X occurs in English in exactly n ways: $X_1, X_2, ..., X_n$.

(ii) Linguistic phenomenon Y cannot occur in English.

These assertions will not be proved, in the sense that a mathematical or scientific assertion might be proved, for they cannot be. So, when I say (i) or (ii), what I really mean is this:

Rush on into the Aramis counter . . . now!
Discover Aramis 900,
the revolutionary grooming system for men.
Our trained Aramis consultant
will take you through the 900
systems programmer first,
after you recieve a complementary
bottle of herbal after shave.[29]

5.6.1. The focus of temporal anaphors

Linguists have spent considerable time analyzing time and tense, and in recent years a few AI workers have examined the problems of computer understanding and representation of temporal concepts and temporal reference in natural language (Bruce 1972; Cohen 1976; Kahn and Gorry 1977; Sondheimer 1977a, 1977b). Strangely, AI workers have not considered temporal anaphora. My discussion below will assume the availability of an understander for non-anaphoric temporal references. I will show that temporal anaphors — the temporally

---

(iii)Although I've thought about it quite a bit, neither I, in my capacity as a native speaker of Australian English, nor anyone else I've asked (if any), can come up with an example of well-formed English text in which X_p $(p>n)$ or Y occurs.

It is possible, therefore, that X_p $(p>n)$ or Y may in fact occur in English, perhaps even rampantly — the language after all is infinite — but has managed to avoid my investigations. Maybe you, faithful reader, can easily come up with an example of X_p or Y. If so, I would be interested in seeing it.

The problem here is that of the "boundary of language". Wilks (1975c) expresses the situation well:

"Suppose that tomorrow someone produces what appears to be the complete AI understanding system, including of course all the right inference rules to resolve all the pronoun references in English. We know in advance that many ingenious and industrious people would immediately sit down and think up examples of perfectly acceptable texts that were not covered by those rules. We know they would be able to do this, just as surely as we know that if someone were to show us a boundary line to the universe and say 'you cannot step over this', we would promptly do so.

Do not misunderstand my point here: it is not that I would consider the one who offered the rule system as refuted by such an example, particularly if the latter took time and ingenuity to construct. On the contrary, it is the counterexample methodology that is refuted."

Because language is inherently infinite, one cannot prove the non-occurrence of X_p $(p>n)$ or Y by enumeration of all possible sentences. And, a fortiori, it is claimed by some (such as Wilks 1971, 1973a, 1975c) that a natural language cannot even be understood or generated by a finite set of rules; that almost ANYTHING can be understood by a human's language system, provided it is accompanied by enough context or explanation. Thus a language understanding system cannot be refuted on the basis of a counterexample, provided its level of performance is by some criterion adequate, for a counterexample could be generated for ANY system we could ever possibly construct; and therefore we need special rules and recovery mechanisms to handle these counterexamples. While I am not convinced that this view is entirely correct (I discuss it further in Hirst (1976a)), it is not unappealling. What it means to us for the present is that the method of argument expressed in (iii) is the best we can do here.

[29]Advertisement for David Jones' department store in: *The Canberra times*, 21 June 1977, page 1. Spelling, punctuation and temporal location are as supplied.

relative phrases and certain uses of the word *then* that we saw in section 2.3.11 – refer to the "temporal location" of the preceding text, and that discourse structure and topic have little to do with such anaphors.

By the TEMPORAL LOCATION of a text, I simply mean the time at which the actions being described take place. This time may be specified explicitly, as in (5-53), or not, as in (5-54):

> (5-53) After dinner, Ross retired to the bathroom with a copy of *Time*, while Nadia and Sue played cribbage. [after dinner]

> (5-54) Nadia dropped the orange down the chute, fervently hoping for a miracle. [the time when Nadia, while hoping fervently for a miracle, dropped the orange down the chute]

The text in brackets after each example represents its temporal location.

Not all text has a temporal location. Some present-tense sentences are effectively tenseless in that they refer to "all eternity"; this case occurs, for example, when discussing abstract ideas, as in (5-55):

> (5-55) Some present-tense sentences are effectively tenseless in that they refer to "all eternity"; this case occurs, for example, when discussing abstract ideas, as in (5-55).

Clearly, detecting tenselessness requires inference on the meaning of the text.[30] Tenseless texts do not, in general, involve temporal anaphors, except when describing repeated actions over time:

> (5-56) On Saturdays at the Enver Hoxha Christian Gospel Commune, we always follow the same inspiring schedule. Reveille is sounded at six am, and the residents eat a hearty breakfast of hash-brown potato peels. The next two hours are spent in quiet meditation and prayer, and it is then that glossolalia sometimes occurs.

The referent of any temporal anaphor is always the most recent temporal location of the text. For example, in (5-56) the antecedent of *the next two hours* is the time the residents have breakfast, and of *then* is the two hours of meditation. I have been unable to construct any well-formed text which

---

[30]Some languages allow a lexical disambiguation. For example, in Spanish the verb *to be* is *ser* if tenseless and *estar* if not; compare (i) and (ii):

(i) Soy australiano. [I am an Australian.]
(ii) Estoy enfermo. [I am sick.]

[31]One possible exception occurs when two times are contrasted as in (i):

(i) Surely their plane is more likely to arrive on Tuesday than on Wednesday. If we want to meet them, we should go to the airport THEN.

This sentence, in which *then* is stressed and intended to be temporally anaphoric, was acceptable only to a small proportion of informants, who understood *then* as meaning Tuesday. (There was no general consensus among informants as to whether or not (i) was either gram-

violates this general rule.[31] Temporal cataphors are not possible.[32]

The problem then becomes one of establishing a temporal location for the text. This is one aspect of the problem that Bruce, Cohen, and Kahn and Gorry, in the work cited above, approached, and it is not appropriate to discuss it here — the interested reader should see the work mentioned — except for two points:

First, time tends to move forward in the discourse, as in this example:

(5-57) Nadia filled the kettle, put it on the stove, and busied herself with the task of icing the cake. Suddenly, the telephone rang.

Although there are no explicit indications in the text, when reading it we have no trouble in deciding that the four events described took place one after the other in this order:

1 Nadia fills the kettle.
2 Nadia puts the kettle on the stove.
3 Nadia commences icing the cake.
4 The telephone rings.

The assumption of discourse cohesion implies further that these events took place contiguously (when viewed at a certain level of detail). This is the default case, and variations from it must be explicitly flagged.[33] This means that the temporal location is constantly changing in text. Thus in (5-56), the referent of *the next two hours* is not six am precisely, but six am plus the time taken in breakfast plus some certain amount of time taken in relevant overheads (like getting out of bed). (Kahn and Gorry attempt to handle the natural inexactitude of temporal reference with an explicit "FUZZ" element in their representation.)

---

matical or meaningful. When I first tried it without the phrase *if we want to meet them*, some informants understood the referent to be Wednesday and the intent of the speaker to be AVOIDING meeting the plane.) This could be another example of a case in which stress on an anaphor is to be interpreted as meaning *the intended referent is not the one this word would normally have* (see section 7.1 on the effects of stress and intonation).

[32]In Hirst (1976b) I described (i) as temporally cataphoric (and, a fortiori, as a prototype of the only possible temporal cataphor):

(i) #It was <u>then</u>, when Sue had given up all hope, that it began to rain fish.

I no longer believe this to be cataphoric. Rather, *then* here refers to the temporal location of the previous text, and the embedded clause is an expansion on that same temporal location rather than a cataphoric referent for *then*. When presented without preceding text, as it is here, (i) is not coherent, as it presumes a previous temporal context. This could be acceptable as a literary device at the start of a story (cf footnote 5 of Chapter 4).

[33]If variations from the default are not flagged, the result is ill-formed; hence (i) sounds strange:

(i) #I wanna hold you till I die,
Till we both break down and cry.
[From: Hill, Dan. Sometimes when we touch. On: Hill, Dan. *Longer fuse*. LP recording, GRT 9230-1073.]

(One informant told me that they interpreted *die* metaphorically, and thereby restored forward sequential ordering to (i).)

5.6.1 The focus of temporal anaphors

Second, topic is relevant to temporal anaphora only insofar as it affects temporal location; a new topic will usually have a new temporal location. But sometimes a temporal anaphor will explicitly refer across a topic shift to establish the new location by relating it to that of the previous topic.

5.6.2. The focus of locative anaphors

The anaphor *there* and locative relations exactly parallel *then* and temporal relations in that they refer to what we shall (ambiguously) call a text's PHYSICAL LOCATION.[34] An example:

> (5-58) The Church of Scientology met in a secret room behind the local Colonel Sanders' chicken stand. Sue had her first dianetic experience there[1]. Across the street was a McDonald's where The Church Of God The Utterly Indifferent had their meetings, and Ross went there[2] instead, because of the free Big Macs they gave to recent converts.

The referent of *there*[1] is the secret room behind the local Colonel Sanders stand, and the referent of *across the street* is either the secret room or the chicken stand — there is no semantic difference.[35] The McDonald's is the referent of *there*[2].

Determining a text's physical location is quite a different task from finding its temporal location, as there is no locative equivalent to tense in English (nor in any other language, as far as I am aware), nor does text automatically move through space as it does time. Determining physical location therefore relies solely on understanding locative references in the text. A complicating factor in doing this is that a text may have a separate *here*-location — the place where the speaker/writer is producing the text. This requires understanding the text to the extent of being able to determine whether a locative reference applies to the first person or not. For example, in (5-59):

> (5-59) Ross is in Canberra, while I am in Vancouver. In July it is warmer here than there.

---

[34]Also parallelling temporal reference are the problematic contrastive usage and the impossibility of locative cataphora. Texts (i) and (ii) correspond exactly to the examples in footnotes 31 and 32:

> (i) Surely they are more likely to go to Spuzzum than Vancouver. We should wait for them THERE.
> (ii) It was there, where Sue had given up all hope, that the pile of dead fish lay rotting.

[35]This suggests the possibility of a similar text in which there IS a semantic difference, and hence whose physical location is not uniquely determined. I have not, however, found a well-formed example of this.

one must be able to work out that *here* is Vancouver and *there* is Canberra.[36]

---

[36]Text also has a *now*-location in time which parallels its *here*-location, and which an NLU system may have to distinguish from other temporal locations in the text.

5.6.2 The focus of locative anaphors

Chapter 6

CONSTRAINTS AND DEFAULTS IN ANAPHOR RESOLUTION

There is, of course, no firm dividing line between the act of deciding what the candidates for an anaphor's antecedent are and the act of deciding among them; it all depends on how much information there is to limit the possibilities during the search. We can imagine at one extreme a two-pass system which computes when necessary, or always maintains, a focus as we have discussed above, and then chooses among them when necessary, and at the other extreme a one-pass system which applies both focus and anaphor-specific constraints to each entity when looking for a particular referent. Combination approaches are also possible. I know of no evidence favouring one of these approaches over the others on theoretical grounds, nor is it clear when each is the most computationally efficient.

So far in this thesis, I have tacitly assumed that in determining the candidates — the focus — we have no information about a particular anaphor occurrence, but are rather generating the maximal set of entities that some anaphor could refer to at the present point in the text. In this chapter, now, I consider the additional constraints imposed by having information on a particular anaphor that needs resolving, and the problem of default referents. It is unimportant to the present discussion at what point anaphor-specific information is used.

Many anaphor-specific factors have been discussed earlier in this thesis; in these cases, the reader is referred back to the appropriate sections.

6.1. Gender and number

While gender and number are strong constraints on reference, we saw in section 2.3.1 that they are not absolute: a plural anaphor can have a singular antecedent, a feminine one a masculine antecedent, and so forth.

6.2. Syntactic constraints

Linguists have discovered many syntactic constraints on anaphoric reference; see section 3.2.2.

6.3. Inference and world knowledge

In sections 2.4.2 and 3.2.6, we saw how world knowledge and inference may need to be applied.

6.4. Parallelism

Consider the following texts:

(6-1) Ross likes his[(1)] beer and Daryel his[(2)] carrot juice, but Bruce swears by his[(3)] Samoa Fogcutter (two parts gin, one part red wine).

(6-2) Roger makes some great drinks at home. Ross likes his[(1)] beer and Daryel his[(2)] carrot juice, but Bruce swears by his[(3)] Samoa Fogcutter.

In each *his* refers to the immediately preceding name, and in the additional context of (6-2), each refers to Roger. That each *his* is dealt with in the same way, in a certain sense, is the not uncommon linguistic phenomenon PARALLELISM. Parallelism can operate at both the syntactic and semantic levels. Its effects are quite strong: there is, I conjecture, NO context in which can be embedded such that the *his*s aren't dealt with in a parallel manner (in which *his* [(1)] is someone in a previous sentence, *his* [(2)] is Daryel, and *his* [(3)] is Ross, for example).

Clearly, an anaphor resolver needs a knowledge of parallelism, although I am not aware of any attempt to formalize the phenomenon, let alone implement it. Note that parallelism is particularly important in resolving surface count anaphora (see section 2.3.2).

6.5. The preferred antecedent and plausibility

In section 2.6, when discussing the problems of ambiguous text, I introduced the notion of a PREFERRED or DEFAULT ANTECEDENT. The preferred antecedent rule says "If you cannot decide on a single 'right' antecedent for the reference, choose from the uneliminated candidates the one that has quality X in the greatest proportion; if no candidate has significantly more of quality X than the others, treat the sentence as genuinely ambiguous". In this section, I will look at the nature of quality X, and will start by immediately prejudicing the discussion by giving X the name PLAUSIBILITY.

Let us first recall two potentially ambiguous examples from section 2.6:

(6-3)   Daryel told Ross he[1] was the ugliest person he[2] knew of.

(6-4)   The FBI's role is to ensure our country's freedom and be ever watchful of those who threaten it.

The default interpretation of (6-3) is that Daryel is insulting Ross ($he^{(1)}$ = *Ross*,
$he^{(2)}$ = *Daryel*), rather than being self-critical ($he^{(1)}$ = $he^{(2)}$ = *Daryel*). This may
be simply because insulting behaviour is more common than openly self-critical
behaviour with respect to personal appearance in western English-speaking cul-
tures. That is, an insult is the most plausible interpretation of (6-3), and the
corresponding antecedents are chosen accordingly. Similarly, in (6-4), *it* is
more plausibly *our country* or *our country's freedom* than *the FBI* or *the FBI's
role*.

Moreover, Kirby (1977, 1979) has shown in psycholinguistic experiments
that plausibility of meaning is a factor in the time taken to understand a struc-
turally ambiguous sentence — ambiguous sentences lacking a single, obviously
most plausible interpretation take longer. This suggests that plausibility could
also be relevant to ambiguous anaphors.[1]

Plausibility differs from other constraints mostly in its weakness. For
example, the gender constraints that make (6-5) so bad:

(6-5)   *Sue found himself pregnant.

can be broken in certain cases (see 2.3.1), but in most contexts are very strong
and not really a matter of degree. Plausibility, on the other hand, IS a matter
of degree, and always requires evaluation relative to the other possibilities.

Is plausibility the only factor (other than theme, of course) in assigning the
default antecedent? Or conversely, is there a well-formed anaphorically ambiguous text in which a preferred antecedent exists but is neither the theme nor
the candidate that gives the text its most plausible reading? I have not been
able to construct such an example, but am not willing to assert that none exist.
If they do exist, they are probably rare enough for an NLU to ignore with reasonable impunity.

The computational problem of deciding how plausible an alternative is, is
extremely difficult. While it relies on knowledge of real-world norms, inference
plays a part too. For example, one is unlikely to find explicitly in a knowledge-
base grounds on which (6-4) can be resolved, namely:

(6-6)   If X guards Y, then it makes more sense for X to keep under sur-
veillance all who threaten Y rather than just those who threaten X.

Working out what "makes most sense" can involve an extremely complex and
time-consuming process of generating and evaluating consequences.

However, there is at least one form in which plausibility becomes computationally simple, and we shall examine this in the next section.

---

[1]It remains for someone to perform a properly controlled experiment to test this hypothesis.
But see also the next section, on causal valence.

6.5 The preferred antecedent and plausibility

6.6. Implicit verb causality

One guise in which plausibility turns up is IMPLICIT VERB CAUSALITY or CAUSAL VALENCE. In a series of experiments (Garvey and Caramazza 1974; Garvey, Caramazza and Yates 1975; Caramazza, Grober, Garvey and Yates 1977), it was shown by Catherine Garvey and her colleagues that the causal valence of a verb can affect the antecedents assigned to nearby anaphors. For example, consider these texts (from Caramazza et al 1977):

(6-7) Muriel won the money from Helen because <u>she</u> was a skillful player.

(6-8) Ronald scolded Joe because <u>he</u> was annoying.

People tend to interpret *she* in (6-7) as *Muriel*, the first NP of the sentence, and *he* in (6-8) as *Joe*, the second NP. In general, with sentences of the form:

(6-9) *NP1 VERB*ed *NP2* because {he | she} . . .

(where both *NP1* and *NP2* are of the same gender as the pronoun) there is a distinct tendency for people to construct and interpret the sentence such that the pronoun refers to *NP1* in the case of some verbs, and *NP2* in the case of some others. (Some verbs are neutral.) The strength of this tendency is the verb's causal valence.

Garvey et al (1975) determined the causal valence of a number of verbs by asking subjects to complete sentence fragments in the form of (6-9) with a suitable reason for the action described therein; to distract them from the potential ambiguity, subjects were told that the experiment was about people's motivations, and apparently the subjects performed the task unaware of the ambiguity. For each verb, the proportion of responses favouring *NP2* as the referent was defined to be its causal valence. In a subsequent experiment (Caramazza et al 1977) it was found that subjects took longer to comprehend sentences such as this:

(6-10) Patricia won the money from Janet because <u>she</u> was a careless player.

where semantics force an interpretation contrary to the usual causal valence of the verb.

We can see that if an NLU system had the implicit causality of each verb marked in its lexicon, this information could be used to help find the preferred antecedent in potentially ambiguous cases.[2]

The phenomenon of causal valence may be explained as simply being a special effect of plausibility. The causal valence data in Garvey et al (1975), Caramazza et al (1977) and Grober, Beardsley and Caramazza (1978) suggest that verbs with an *NP2* bias are exactly those describing an action normally

---

[2]The similar constraints which verbs of introspective experience place on anaphors could also be included; see Springston (1976) and Caramazza et al (1977).

performed in response to an external cause, while *NP1*-biased verbs describe an initiating action.

So, for example, in (6-11), where the verb is *NP1*-biased:

(6-11) Ross apologized to Daryel because <u>he</u>...

it is most likely that Ross has initiated the action — the cause lies with him — and so he is the actor in the subordinate clause, and hence in turn probably the referent of its surface subject. On the other hand, in the case of (6-12) with an *NP2*-biased verb:

(6-12) Ross scolded Daryel because <u>he</u>...

it is most likely that Ross is responding to something Daryel has done, and hence the cause lies with Daryel. It follows that a text like (6-13), in which it is hard to determine the initiator with any confidence, is more ambiguous than one in which there is an actor who is clearly the initiator:

(6-13) Ross telephoned Daryel because <u>he</u> wanted an apology.

Unfortunately, the nice computability of implicit causality does not seem to generalize; with the exception of interrogativization (Garvey et al 1975) and certain strong modal verbs (Grober et al 1978), most linguistic variations on the "pure" form of (6-9), such as negation, passivization or the use of *but* instead of *because*, tend to attenuate the effect of *NP2*-biased verbs, moving them towards *NP1*. It is possible that analogous measures may be found that apply in different contexts from (6-9). However, unless these contexts are rather general, such measures are of little use; indeed, one wonders if enough sentences of the form of (6-9) are ever encountered to make the inclusion of implicit causality in an NLU system a worthwhile endeavour.

6.7. Semantic distance

To check for the possibility of an antecedent being non-identically related to a referent (see section 2.4.2), the SEMANTIC DISTANCE between the referent and its candidate antecedents needs to be considered. The semantic distance between two concepts or entities is simply a metric of how "similar" they are. If a candidate is within a certain threshold semantic distance of the referent, then the possibility that it is an antecedent must be considered.

How to compute a semantic distance and set a threshold are major research problems that underlie much of the research in anaphora understanding. In sections 5.2, 5.3 and 5.5 we saw approaches in which a knowledge representation was used to provide a measure of semantic distance. However, as we saw in 2.4.2, computing the semantic distance relationship may involve complex inference, and no-one has yet attempted a general solution.

Chapter 7

THE LAST CHAPTER

This chapter is a miscellany. In the first three sections, I discuss some residual points and issues raised by the previous chapters. I then list some of the interesting problems that remain, and conclude with some appropriate remarks.

7.1. Anaphora in spoken language

In spoken English, vocal stress can be used to change the intended referent of an anaphor. For example, in this sentence (with normal stress) Ross gives Daryel both the measles and the mumps:

(7-1) Ross gave Daryel the measles, and then <u>he</u> gave <u>him</u> the mumps.

However, when the anaphors are stressed the meaning is reversed so that Ross gets the mumps:

(7-2) Ross gave Daryel the measles, and then <u>HE</u> gave <u>HIM</u> the mumps.

In effect the stress indicates that the referent of the anaphor is not the one you would normally choose but rather the next choice.

The principle may explain why (2-52)[1] works. If *one* ϕ were unstressed,[2] it would clearly albeit nonsensically refer to *father*. The stress indicates that a different referent must be found, and the only place another referent can be found is "inside" the anaphoric island *father*.

For more discussion of the relationship between anaphora and intonation, see Akmajian and Jackendoff (1970) and Akmajian (1973).

---

[1](2-52) Ross is already a father THREE TIMES OVER, but Clive hasn't even had ONE ϕ yet.

[2]Note here the interesting concept of stressing an ellipsis.

7.2. Anaphora in computer language generation

7.2.1. Introduction

Although much effort has been expended towards the understanding of natural language by computer, relatively little work has been done on the converse problem of generating a surface text from some internal meaning representation. Such generation is however necessary, for example in machine translation systems that use a language-independent intermediate representation.

Among the many unresolved issues in language generation is how best to describe an entity, and to what extent, including anaphorization, the description may be abbreviated. For example, consider (7-3) and (7-4) (based on an example from McDonald (1978b:69)), which are intended to convey the same message:

> (7-3) Because of the Sangrail crisis, Ross asked Daryel to cancel his meeting with the Lesotho delegation.

> (7-4) Because of the hullabaloo resulting from the theft of the Sangrail, Ross asked Daryel to cancel Ross's meeting with some people from Lesotho who had been going to inspect our taxidermy research section.

The difference between these texts is that the first is designed for an audience familiar with the people and basic issues involved, while the second is not. The first might be spoken to a co-worker, the second to a stranger met a cocktail party. In each case, different descriptions are chosen for some entities, and (7-4) avoids a pronoun which is ambiguous without knowledge of the people involved, in this case that Daryel is Ross's secretary who schedules his boss's activities.

In its most general form, description formation is an extremely difficult task, requiring the speaker to have a detailed model of the listener. In practice, so far, designers of computational systems have not used such a model, nor even given much attention to the problem; Goldman's BABEL (Goldman 1974, 1975; Schank, Goldman, Rieger and Riesbeck 1975), for example, apparently had only very primitive heuristics for description and pronominalization (though Goldman did address other important issues in the word-choice problem). Grosz (1978) and Ortony (1978) discuss some issues in generation of descriptions. To my knowledge, the only study of anaphora from the viewpoint of computational generation of language is that of David McDonald. The next sub-section is a brief description of this work.

7.2.2. Structural constraints on subsequent reference

McDonald (1978b) addresses the issue of anaphor generation, which is more constrained by syntax and sentence structure than the generation of initial reference to an entity. He describes how these constraints are used by a computer program which generates an English sentence from a tree representation based on predicate calculus. (For an overview of the program and the representation, see McDonald (1978a).)

The generation process is done in one pass without back-up. (This mirrors people's inability to unspeak the earlier words of a sentence as they generate the later ones.) When it is necessary to make reference to an element, a list of message elements mentioned so far is consulted to see if the present one has been previously referenced. If it has, a set of pronominalization heuristics are applied. First come quick checks such as whether the element has been pronominalized before. If these are unable to decide for or against pronominalization, more detailed examination takes place, and the syntactic or structural relationship between the present instance and the previous instance, such as whether they are in the same simple sentence or not, is computed.

This relationship is then used by a set of heuristics which determine whether there are any nearby "distracting references" which would cause ambiguity if pronominalization occurs. Ideally, this requires a model of the listener's knowledge; for the present, McDonald's program relies on testing the "pronominalizability" of the current element and possible distractors, and does not pronominalize if any distractor scores highest. Pronominalizability is measured simply as the weighted count of the number of pronominalization heuristics that apply to that element at that point in the text.

If an element is not rendered as a pronoun, the program must find the simplest description which will distinguish it from possible distractors. Often it is sufficient to use a definite determiner, *the* or *that*, with the head noun of a descriptive NP. See McDonald (1978b:70-71) for details.

McDonald hopes to add pragmatic and rhetorical considerations to his program. This would include using the notion of a focus or theme, pronominalization of which would usually be obligatory.

7.2.3. Conclusion

Research in anaphor generation is lagging behind that in anaphor understanding, and this is perhaps not surprising. A properly generated anaphor is one that may be quickly and easily understood, suggesting that the generator needs to consider how its audience will resolve the anaphor. It follows that the development of a proper anaphor generation system will require first the development of a full anaphor resolution system.

7.3. Well-formedness judgements

A persistent theme that has kept resurfacing throughout this thesis is the problem of knowing whether or not a sentence is well-formed. I have complained about texts alleged to prove points about the English language which are probably not English at all (see footnote 8 of Chapter 4), and about feeble attempts (my own included) to avoid this problem merely by verifying texts with a couple of readily-available informants.

It seems to me that nothing short of psychological testing is adequate to determine the relative well-formedness of a text about which there is even the slightest doubt. Language is, after all, a psychological phenomenon, and surely no-one in these modern times believes that well-formedness is a binary value engraved indelibly on a text and known to every competent speaker of the language. In fact well-formedness is a matter of degree, and no two people speak exactly the same language. It follows, therefore, that a well-formedness judgement, if meaningful at all, must represent the unbiased consensus of a number of speakers of the language.

Since the demand characteristics (Orne 1962) of informal enquiries will bias the results, it is necessary to obtain other people's judgements in a formal experiment, well controlled for influences that could bias subjects. This kind of experiment is well known in psycholinguistics; one example that we've already seen was in determining the causal valence of some verbs (see section 6.6). It is often claimed that linguistics is just a branch of psychology. Artificial intelligence is too. And both linguistics and AI need to use the experimental methods of psychology to substantiate their claims about human linguistic behaviour, upon which their theories are based.

What kind of experiment constitutes an adequate test of a sentence's well-formedness? I think that a simple speeded binary choice test would do: Subjects, told that the experiment is to determine how fast people can tell if a sentence is grammatical and meaningful, are presented with test sentences, intermixed with distractors, on a display. They have to judge the sentence and press a YES or NO key as fast as possible.[3] The proportion of subjects pushing the YES button would be a measure of each sentence's well-formedness.

You will by now be wondering if I really think that such a procedure should be carried out for each and every *John can run* sentence used as an example in the literature. After all, you object, while there are undoubtedly dubious texts for which the procedure is necessary, we highly educated and literate researchers are expert at determining what a language community, our own at least, will accept. Every time we write a sentence, whether it be an example in a linguistic argument or not, we check it for well-formedness, with almost invariable success. So why shouldn't we trust our own judgements?

My rejoinder to this is that determining the well-formedness of a text in support of a linguistic argument is not the same as determining the well-formedness of sentences used for normal communication. In the former case, one usually has the linguistic argument first and then works backward trying to

---

[3]This experimental procedure has been used by several researchers in psycholinguistics.

find a text which supports the point and which contains no obfuscating factors. And then, as we have seen, it is all too easy to come up with an ill-formed text without being aware of it, even if that text is as simple as, for example, (4-9)[4] Recall, too, that linguists' intuitions of well-formedness are different from those of normal people (Spencer 1973) and vary according to mood (Carroll and Bever 1978).[5] Even if the linguistic argument is inspired by an unusual real-world text, it is well to verify that this text is not unusual merely by reason of being subtly ill-formed.

I do not, of course, expect a new experimental rigour to take linguistics by storm, even though I think most people would agree with my arguments, for most linguists have neither the facilities nor the inclination to start performing experiments. A useful compromise would be a service to which linguists could send the key texts on which their arguments lie for well-formedness testing for a moderate fee.[6][7]

> *Write a function TRANSLATE which translates the input*
> *from English to a LISP form.*
> — *Alan Keith Mackworth*[8]

7.4. Research problems

This is the traditional suggestions-for-further-research section. In it, I present some questions that remain unanswered, tasks that remain undone, exercises that the reader may find amusing. For each, the section number(s) in parentheses indicate where in this thesis the matter is discussed further.

The study of language and reference:
- (1.1) Is an implementation a theory?
- (1.2) How do words denote concepts?
- (1.1) Can we define a (domain-independent) Habitable English for database queries? (Habitable English is to grammar, semantics and pragmatics as Basic English is to vocabulary.) Is there a simple formula, similar to those

---

[4](4-9) John left the window and drank the wine on the table. It was brown and round.

[5]Moreover, I have occasionally been surprised by the poor linguistic abilities and/or minimal communicative competence of some of AI's "amateur linguists".

[6]World-wide franchises are now available. Contact the author for details.

[7]Nothing in this section is to be construed as belittling the important theoretical aspects of linguistics. One reader of a draft of this section suggested that just as experimental physics needs theoretical physics, so linguistics needs the important insights gained from theoretical work which cannot be supplanted by any amount of experiment. This is true. However theoretical physics has its theories tested by experimental physics. My complaint is that linguistic theories are often accepted without any attempt at experimental verification, and this is a Bad Thing.

[8]Part of an assignment for third-year UBC Computer Science students learning LISP, 17 November 1978.

used to determine the readability of a text, which could measure habitability without recourse to performing real-world experiments with the language subset?

- (3.2.7) Write a book discussing issues in the relationship between the nature of language generation and understanding, and the structure of the human mind.
- (4.2) How do oenologists communicate?
- (5.6) Can natural language be understood by a system using a finite set of rules, or a finite set of rules for generating a possibly infinite set of rules?
- (7.3) Write a critique of my remarks on the need to psychologically test the well-formedness of sample texts, presenting an opposing view.
- (7.3) Buy a sample text testing service franchise from the author, and see if it proves to be useful and/or profitable. Has your service influenced linguists' attitudes to sample texts?

Anaphora, anaphors and antecedents:

- (2.1) Can the set of implicit antecedents that texts can evoke be formally defined? What may be an implicit antecedent, and under what circumstances? Consider especially antecedents for verb phrase ellipsis.
- (2.3.1) Formalize the conditions under which *same* can be used as an anaphor.
- (2.3.2) Formalize rules for the generation and analysis of surface count anaphors.
- (2.3.7) Come up with an elegant theory explaining all usages of the non-referential *it*. Explain why sentence (iv) of footnote 38 of Chapter 2 seems ill-formed.
- (2.4.2, 6.7) What non-inferred reference relations are possible? What is to be done about semantic distance?
- (2.6, 6.5, 6.6) Investigate default antecedents. Are they affected by any factors other than plausibility and theme? How do they relate to verb causality?
- (6.4) Formalize rules for syntactic and semantic parallelism.
- (6.5) How can plausibility of a candidate antecedent be efficiently measured computationally?
- (6.6) Are causal valence data of any computational use? Can the concept of causal valence be usefully generalized?
- (7.1) In what ways can stress on an ellipsis be phonetically realized?

Anaphora resolution systems:

- (3.1.6) How may an anaphor resolver best be evaluated? Prepare a standard corpus of text, which includes all types of anaphora and reference both easy and hard, and make it available to people who want independent test data for their theories or systems.
- (3.1.6) Beef up Hobbs's algorithm so that it works even more frequently.

- (3.2.3) Can an anaphor resolver do without heuristics?

Focus and discourse theme:

- (3.2.1) Should there be one large focus set, or should focus be divided up into noun types, verb types, etc? What is the best such division?

- (4.1 passim) Define the concepts of theme, rheme, topic, comment, given and new so definitively that everyone will use your definitions.

- (4.1 passim) How can the local and global theme of an arbitrary text be determined computationally?

- (4.2, 5 passim) What exactly IS the relationship between theme and focus?

- (6) To what extent should a focus be computed independent of any anaphor that needs resolution?

Current approaches to anaphora and focus:

- (5.1) Generalize the concept of secondary competence. Is there any psycholinguistic evidence that linguistic competence and/or verbal ability comes in well-defined layers? Are some people more prone to generating inconsiderate anaphors than others? Do such people actually find inconsiderate pronouns easier to understand than other people do? Could there be a consistently different model of language in such people?

- (5.1.1, 5.1.2, 7.3) Test Kantor's assertions about pronoun comprehension through experiments such as observation of readers' eye movements and/or reaction-time measurement.

- (5.1.1) What factors affect the activatedness of a concept?

- (5.1.2) How do we know when a concept occurs only as a descriptor and not "in its own right"?

- (5.2.1) Are there other common sorts of dialogue which are as highly structured as task-oriented dialogues? How can their structures be exploited?

- (5.2.2) How could Grosz's methods be applied to the resolution of pronouns?

- (5.2.2, 5.3.3) Given a sentence in a vacuous context which sets up a theme or focus for the interpretation of subsequent sentences, how may this theme be discovered? That is, how is an initial focus determined?

- (5.2.2, 5.3.3) Analyze and classify various clues to focus shift, and give rules for their detection. If more than one is indicated, how is the conflict resolved?

- (5.1.2, 5.2.3, 5.5) Can Grosz's mechanisms be generalized?

- (5.2.1, 5.3) Is focus, the repository of antecedents, really identical to the focus of attention or the discourse topic? If not, under what conditions are they identical?

- (5.3.2) How can a language understander decide when a difficult reference can be left unresolved without engendering problems later on?

- (5.3.4) What is the relation between the genericity of an anaphor and its antecedent?

- (5.4.1) Formalize a complete solution to the intrasentential anaphor resolution problem in Webber's formalism.
- (5.4.2) How may a *one*-anaphor be reliably recognized?
- (5.4.2) Are all antecedents of *one*-anaphors textually recent? Under what conditions are textually recent descriptions not available as antecedents?
- (5.4.2) Find the general principle by which strained anaphors can be resolved.
- (5.4.2) Under what conditions can list elements be abstracted into an antecedent for a *one*-anaphor?
- (5.4.3) How may inference be used with Webber's formalism so that verb phrase ellipsis triggers that are not textually similar to the elided VP may be detected?
- (5.4.4) To what extent does Webber's formalism need the addition of discourse pragmatics? How could they be provided?
- (5.5) Can scripts or frames be made suitable for the understanding of free or deviant discourse?
- (5.5.1) What is the "right" set of discourse coherence relations *(a)* for anaphor resolution, and *(b)* for general NLU? Define them rigorously.
- (5.5.1) Can a set of primitive coherence relations for building more complex relations be defined? Be sure to give the rules under which the primitives may combine.
- (5.5.1) What is the best level — clause, sentence or paragraph — to handle discourse cohesion?
- (5.5.3) Is the search order for a node for feasible connection in Lockman's (1978) CRRA always optimal? Can it lead to error?
- (5.5.3) Can Lockman's CRRA be sure all referable entities are considered?
- (5.5.3) Can the sub-tree of a complex sentence always be determined syntactically? Look for counterexamples to Lockman's table look-up procedure.
- (5.5.3) Devise and implement a judgement mechanism for Lockman's CRRA.
- (5.6.1) How can the temporal location of a text be determined?
- (5.6.1) Under what conditions can a tenseless text contain temporal anaphors?
- (5.6.2) Is there a natural language that has a locative equivalent to tense? (May require field work.)
- (5.6.2, 5.6.1) Is the *now* location of a text ever an obfuscating factor as the *here* location sometimes is?

Anaphora in discourse generation:
- (2.2, 7.2) What sort of model of the listener does a speaker have to have for anaphor generation? What knowledge representation is appropriate for the model? Does the model have psychological reality? How does the model relate to Cohen's (1978) work on models of discourse participants?

7.4 Research problems

- (7.2) Should a discourse generator operate in one pass without back-up?
- (4.1 passim, 7.2) Devise a generative grammar in which local and global theme are explicit elements in the deep representation. Use your model to construct a computational discourse generation program for a machine translation system.
- (7.2) Devise a mechanism which uses an audience model in generating descriptions and anaphors in discourse. Integrate it into the program you constructed in the preceding exercise.

7.5. Conclusion

This thesis has surveyed the problem of computational understanding of anaphora and attempts at a solution thereof. We have seen that an adequate solution to the problem will require the use of discourse pragmatics and the notion of theme to maintain a focus. We have further seen that a complete solution, in which all reference relations, including those determined by inference, are recovered is extremely difficult, and the surface has yet barely been scratched. The work that remains to be done will influence and be influenced by work in linguistics and artificial intelligence. Anaphora buffs have an exciting time ahead.

> *English has no anaphors and the whole notion of anaphora has simply been a popular fallacy.*
> — *William C Watt (1973:469)*

REFERENCES (Bibliographic)

I think, sir, since you care for the advice of an old man,
sir, you will find it a very good practice always to verify
your references, sir!
    — *Martin Joseph Routh[1]*

AKMAJIAN, Adrian (1973). The role of focus in the interpretation of anaphoric expressions. in: Stephen Robert Anderson and René Paul Viktor Kiparsky (editors). *A Festschrift for Morris Halle.* New York: Holt, Rinehart and Winston, 1973, 215-226.

AKMAJIAN, Adrian and HENY, Frank W (1975). *An introduction to the principles of transformational syntax.* Cambridge, Massachusetts: MIT Press, 1975.

AKMAJIAN, Adrian and JACKENDOFF, Ray S (1970). Coreferentiality and stress. *Linguistic inquiry,* *1*(1), 1970, 124-126.

ALLERTON, D J (1978). The notion of 'givenness' and its relations to presupposition and to theme. *Lingua,* *44*(2/3), February/March 1978, 133-168.

ANDERSON, Stephen Robert (1976). Pro-sentential forms and their implications for English sentence structure. [1] in: McCawley 1976, 165-200. [2] also published as: mimeo, Bloomington, Indiana: Indiana University Linguistics Club, 1972.

BARANOFSKY, Sharon (1970). Some heuristics for automatic detection and resolution of anaphora in discourse. Unpublished MSc thesis, Department of Computer Science, University of Texas, Austin, January 1970.

BOBROW, Daniel Gureasko (1964). A question-answering system for high school algebra word problems. *AFIPS conference proceedings,* *26*, FJCC 1964, 591-614.

BODEN, Margaret A (1977). *Artificial intelligence and natural man.* Hassocks: Harvester Press, 1977.

BRANSFORD, John D and JOHNSON, Marcia K (1973). Considerations of some problems of comprehension. in: William G Chase (editor). *Visual information processing,* New York: Academic Press, 1973, 383-438.

BROWSE, Roger Alexander (1976). <Untitled paper on the work of Yorick Wilks>. Unpublished report, Department of Computer Science, University of British Columbia, August 1976.

---

[1]Attributed in: Burgon, John William. *Lives of twelve good men* (new edition). [1] New York: Scribner and Welford, 1891. [2] on microfiche: Louisville: Lost Cause Press, 1975. page 38.

BROWSE, Roger Alexander (1977). A knowledge identification phase of natural language analysis. MSc thesis, Department of Computer Science, University of British Columbia, January 1977.

BROWSE, Roger Alexander (1978). Knowledge identification and metaphor. *Proceedings of the second national conference*, Canadian Society for Computational Studies of Intelligence/Societe canadienne des etudes d'intelligence par ordinateur. Toronto, July 1978, 48-54.

BRUCE, Bertram C (1972). A model for temporal references and its application in a question answering program. *Artificial intelligence.* 3(1), 1972, 1-25.

BULLWINKLE, Candace L. *see also* Sidner, Candace L.

BULLWINKLE, Candace L (1977a). The semantic component of PAL: The personal assistant language understanding program. Working paper 141, Artificial Intelligence Laboratory, Massachusetts Institute of Technology, March 1977.

BULLWINKLE, Candace L (1977b). Levels of complexity in discourse for anaphora disambiguation and speech act interpretation. [1] *Proceedings of the fifth international joint conference on artificial intelligence.* Cambridge, Massachusetts, August 1977, 43-49. [2] an earlier version was published as: Memo 413, Artificial Intelligence Laboratory, Massachusetts Institute of Technology, May 1977.

BUNDY, Alan (1979). *Artificial intelligence: An introductory course.* [1] Elsevier North-Holland, 1979. [2] Edinburgh University Press, 1978.

CARAMAZZA, Alfonso; GROBER, Ellen H; GARVEY, Catherine and YATES, Jack B (1977). Comprehension of anaphoric pronouns. *Journal of verbal learning and verbal behavior, 16*(5), October 1977, 601-609.

CARLSON, Greg N and MARTIN, Larry W (1975). This antecedent isn't the right one. *Glossa, 9*(1), 1975, 13-24.

CARROLL, John M and BEVER, Thomas G (1978). The non-uniqueness of linguistic intuitions. Research report RC6938 (#29749), Thomas J Watson Research Center, IBM, Yorktown Heights, New York, 10 January 1978.

CATON, Charles Edwin (editor) (1963). *Philosophy and ordinary language.* Urbana: University of Illinois Press, 1963.

CHAFE, Wallace L (1970). *Meaning and the structure of language.* The University of Chicago Press, 1970.

CHAFE, Wallace L (1972). Discourse structure and human knowledge. in: Roy O Freedle and John Bissell Carroll (editors). *Language comprehension and the acquisition of knowledge.* Washington: V H Vinton, 1972, 41-70.

CHAFE, Wallace L (1974). Language and consciousness. *Language, 50*(1), 1974, 111-133.

CHAFE, Wallace L (1975). Givenness, contrastiveness, definiteness, subjects, topics and point of view. in: Li 1975, 25-55.

CHARNIAK, Eugene (1972). Toward a model of children's story comprehension. Technical report 266, Artificial Intelligence Laboratory, Massachusetts Institute of Technology, 1972.

CHARNIAK, Eugene (1976). [1] Inference and knowledge. in: Eugene Charniak and Yorick Alexander Wilks (editors). *Computational semantics: An introduction to artificial intelligence and natural language comprehension.* (= Fundamental studies in computer science *4*). Amsterdam: North-Holland, 1976, 1-21 and 129-154. [2] an earlier version of parts of this work was published as: Organization and inference in a frame-like system of common sense knowledge. in: Schank and Nash-Webber 1975, 46-55. [3] another early version was published in: Course notes for a tutorial on computational semantics, given at the Institute for Semantic and Cognitive Studies, Castagnola, Switzerland. 17-22 March 1975. [4] a revised but abbreviated version appears as: Inference and knowledge in language comprehension. *Machine intelligence, 8*, 1977, 541-574.

CHARNIAK, Eugene (1978). With spoon in hand this must be the eating frame. in: Waltz 1978, 187-193.

CHOMSKY, Noam Avram (1957). *Syntactic structures.* (= Janua Linguarum *4*). The Hague: Mouton, 1957.

CHOMSKY, Noam Avram (1965). *Aspects of the theory of syntax.* Cambridge, Massachusetts: MIT Press, 1965.

CLARK, Herbert H (1975). Bridging. in: Schank and Nash-Webber 1975, 188-193.

CLARK, Herbert H and HAVILAND, Susan E (1977). Comprehension and the given-new contract. in: Roy O Freedle (editor). *Discourse production and comprehension.* (= Discourse processes: Advances in research *1*). Norwood New Jersey: Ablex Publishing, 1977.

CLARK, Herbert H and MARSHALL, Catherine (1978). Reference diaries. in: Waltz 1978, 57-63.

COHEN, Philip R (1978). On knowing what to say: Planning speech acts. Technical report 118/PhD thesis, Department of Computer Science, University of Toronto, January 1978.

COHEN, Philip R and PERRAULT, Charles Raymond (1976). Preliminaries for a computer model of conversation. *Proceedings of the first national conference*, Canadian Society for computational studies of intelligence/ Societe canadienne des etudes d'intelligence par ordinateur. Vancouver, British Columbia, August 1976, 102-111.

COHEN, Robin Gail (1976). Computer analysis of temporal reference. Technical report 107, Department of Computer Science, University of Toronto, December 1976.

COLE, Peter and MORGAN, Jerry L (editors) (1975). *Syntax and semantics 3: Speech acts*. New York: Academic Press, 1975.

CORUM, Claudia (1973). Anaphoric peninsulas. *Papers from the ninth regional meeting*, Chicago Linguistic Society, 1973, 89-97.

DAVIDSON, James Edward (1976). An evaluation of conceptual dependency as a representation for language and knowledge. Unpublished report, Department of Computer Science, University of British Columbia, February 1976.

DEUTSCH, Barbara G. see Grosz, Barbara Jean.

DILLER, Timothy C (editor) (1975). Proceedings of the 13th annual meeting, Association for Computational Linguistics. *American journal of computational linguistics*. Microfiche 32-36, 1975.

DONNELLAN, Keith S (1966). Reference and definite descriptions. *Philosophical review*, *LXXV*, July 1966, 281-304.

EDES, E (1968). Output conditions in anaphoric expressions with split antecedents. Unpublished MS, Harvard University, 1968.

EISENSTADT, Marc (1976). Processing newspaper stories: some thoughts on fighting and stylistics. *Proceedings of the AISB summer conference*, Society for the Study of Artificial Intelligence and the Simulation of Behaviour, July 1976, 104-117.

FILLMORE, Charles J (1968). The case for case. in: Emmon Werner Bach and Robert Thomas Harms (editors). *Universals in linguistic theory*. New York: Holt, Rinehart and Winston, 1968, 0-88 [sic].

FILLMORE, Charles J (1972). Deixis I [and] Deixis II. Unpublished lectures, mimeo, 1972.

FILLMORE, Charles J (1977). The case for case reopened. in: Peter Cole and Jerrold M Saddock (editors). *Syntax and semantics 8: Grammatical relations*. New York: Academic Press, 1977, 59-81.

FIRBAS, Jan (1964). On defining the theme in functional sentence analysis. *Travaux linguistiques de Prague*, *1*, 1964, 267-280.

FOWLER, Henry W (1968). *A dictionary of modern English usage* (second edition, revised by sir Ernest Gowers). Oxford University Press, 1968.

FRIEDMAN, Joyce; MORAN, Douglas B and WARREN, David S (1978). Two papers on semantic interpretation in Montague grammar. *American journal of computational linguistics*, microfiche 31, 1978.

GARVEY, Catherine and CARAMAZZA, Alfonso (1974). Implicit causality in verbs. *Linguistic inquiry*, 5(3), Summer 1974, 464-469.

GARVEY, Catherine; CARAMAZZA, Alfonso and YATES, Jack B (1975). Factors influencing assignment of pronoun antecedents. *Cognition*, 3(3), 1974-75, 227-243.

GELBART, Rachel (1976). Generative semantics. Unpublished report, Department of Computer Science, University of British Columbia, 1976.

GIVÓN, Talmy (1975). Topic, pronoun and grammatical agreement. in: Li 1975, 149-188.

GOLDMAN, Neil Murray (1974). Computer generation of language from a deep conceptual base. PhD thesis/AI memo 247, Artificial Intelligence Laboratory, Stanford University, 1974.

GOLDMAN, Neil Murray (1975). Conceptual generation. in: Schank 1975, 289-371.

GOLDSTEIN, Ira P and ROBERTS, R Bruce (1977). NUDGE: A knowledge-based scheduling program. [1] *Proceedings of the fifth international joint conference on artificial intelligence*. Cambridge, Massachusetts, August 1977, 257-263. [2] Memo 405, Artificial Intelligence Laboratory, Massachusetts Institute of Technology, February 1977.

GORDON, David and LAKOFF, George (1971). Conversational postulates. [1] *Papers from the seventh regional meeting*, Chicago Linguistic Society, 1971, 63-84. [2] in: Cole and Morgan 1975, 83-106.

GRICE, H Paul (1975). Logic and conversation. in: Cole and Morgan 1975, 41-58.

GRIMES, Joseph Evans (1975). *The thread of discourse.* [1] (= Janua Linguarum, series minor *207*). The Hague: Mouton, 1975. [2] an incomplete earlier version was published as: Technical report 1, Department of Modern Languages and Linguistics, Cornell University, 1972.

GRINDER, John T and ELGIN, Suzette Haden (1973). *Guide to transformational grammar: History, theory, practice.* New York: Holt, Rinehart and Winston, 1973.

GRINDER, John T and POSTAL, Paul Martin (1971). Missing antecedents. *Linguistic inquiry*, 2(3), Summer 1971, 269-312.

GROBER, Ellen H; BEARDSLEY, William and CARAMAZZA, Alfonso (1978). Parallel function strategy in pronoun assignment. *Cognition*, 6(2), 1978, 117-133.

GROSZ, Barbara Jean (1977a). The representation and use of focus in a system for understanding dialogs. [1] *Proceedings of the fifth international joint conference on artificial intelligence*. Cambridge, Massachusetts, August 1977, 67-76. [2] Technical note 150, Artificial Intelligence Center, SRI

International, June 1977.

GROSZ, Barbara Jean (1977b). The representation and use of focus in dialogue understanding. [1] Unpublished PhD thesis, Department of Computer Science, University of California at Berkeley, June 1977. [2] published, slightly revised, as: Technical note 151, SRI International, Artificial Intelligence Center, July 1977. [3] a newer revised version appears in: Walker 1978, section 4. [4] an earlier version of parts of this work were published in: Walker 1976, chapters VIII-X.

GROSZ, Barbara Jean (1978). Focusing in dialog. [1] in: Waltz 1978, 96-103. [2] Technical note 166, Artificial Intelligence Center, SRI International, July 1978.

HALLIDAY, Michael Alexander Kirkwood (1967). Notes on transitivity and theme in English: Part 2. *Journal of linguistics*, *3*, 1967, 199-244.

HALLIDAY, Michael Alexander Kirkwood and HASAN, Ruqaiya (1976). *Cohesion in English.* (= Longman English Language Series *9*). London: Longman, 1976.

HANKAMER, Jorge (1978). On the nontransformational derivation of some null VP anaphors. *Linguistic inquiry*, *9*(1), Winter 1978, 66-74.

HANKAMER, Jorge and SAG, Ivan A (1976). Deep and surface anaphora. *Linguistic inquiry*, *7*(3), Summer 1976, 391-428.

HARRIS, Larry R (1977). User oriented data base query with the ROBOT natural language query system. *International journal of man-machine studies*, *9*(6), November 1977, 697-713.

HARRIS, Larry R (1978). Status report on the ROBOT natural language query processor. *SIGART newsletter*, number 66, August 1978, 3-4.

HAVILAND, Susan E and CLARK, Herbert H (1974). What's new? Acquiring new information as a process in comprehension. *Journal of verbal learning and verbal behavior*, *13*(5), October 1974, 512-521.

HENDRICKS, William O (1976). *Grammars of style and styles of grammar.* (= North-Holland studies in theoretical poetics *3*). Amsterdam: North-Holland, 1976.

HENDRIX, Gary Grant (1975a). Partitioned networks for the mathematical modeling of natural language semantics. Technical report NL-28, Department of Computer Sciences, University of Texas, Austin, 1975.

HENDRIX, Gary Grant (1975b). Expanding the utility of semantic networks through partitioning. *Advance papers of the fourth international joint conference on artificial intelligence.* Tblisi, Union of Soviet Socialist Republics, September 1975, 115-121.

HENDRIX, Gary Grant (1978). The representation of semantic knowledge. in:

Walker 1978, 121-181

HINDS, John (1977). Paragraph structure and pronominalization. *Papers in linguistics*, *10*(1-2), Spring-Summer 1977, 77-99.

HIRST, Graeme John (1976a). Artificial intelligence and computational linguistics II: Methodology and problems. Unpublished report, Department of Computer Science, University of British Columbia, April 1976.

HIRST, Graeme John (1976b). Anaphora and reference in natural language understanding. Unpublished thesis draft, Department of Computer Science, University of British Columbia, 23 August 1976.

HIRST, Graeme John (1977a). Focus in reference resolution in natural language understanding. Paper presented at the Language and Speech Conference, Melbourne, November 1977.

HIRST, Graeme John (1977b). Cohesive discourse transitions and reference resolution: The cinema metaphor and beyond into the transfinite. Unpublished manuscript, 20 December 1977.

HIRST, Graeme John (1978a). Report on the Conference on Theoretical Issues in Natural Language Processing—2. *AISB quarterly*, number 31, September 1978, 9-11.

HIRST, Graeme John (1978b). A set of primitives for discourse transitions. Unpublishable manuscript, 1 February 1978.

HIRST, Graeme John (1982). Humorous information processing: Why AI must consider humour. In preparation.

HOBBS, Jerry R (1976). [1] Pronoun resolution. Research report 76-1, Department of Computer Sciences, City College, City University of New York, August 1976. [2] an abridged version was published as: Resolving pronoun references. *Lingua*, *44*(4), April 1978, 311-338.

HOBBS, Jerry R (1977). 38 examples of elusive antecedents from published texts. Research report 77-2, Department of Computer Sciences, City College, City University of New York, August 1977.

HOBBS, Jerry R (1978). Coherence and coreference. Technical note 168, Artificial Intelligence Center, SRI International, 4 August 1978.

HORNBY, Peter A (1971). Surface structure and the topic-comment distinction: A developmental study. *Child Development*, *42*, 1971, 1975-1988.

HORNBY, Peter A (1972). The psychological subject and predicate. *Cognitive psychology*, *3*, 1972, 632-642.

HUTCHINS, W J (1978). Machine translation and machine-aided translation. *Journal of documentation*, *34*(2), June 1978, 119-159.

JACOBSEN, Bent (1977). *Transformational-generative grammar*. (= North-Holland Linguistic series *17*). Amsterdam: North-Holland, 1977.

JOHNSON-LAIRD, Philip Nicholas (1968a). The choice of the passive voice in a communicative task. *British journal of psychology, 59*, 1968, 7-15.

JOHNSON-LAIRD, Philip Nicholas (1968b). The interpretation of the passive voice. *Quarterly journal of experimental psychology, 20*, 1968, 69-73.

KAHN, Kenneth and GORRY, G Anthony (1977). Mechanizing temporal knowledge. *Artificial intelligence, 9*(1), August 1977, 87-108.

KANTOR, Robert Neal (1977). The management and comprehension of discourse connection by pronouns in English. PhD thesis, Department of Linguistics, Ohio State University, 1977.

KIERAS, David E (1978). Good and bad structure in simple paragraphs: Effects on apparent theme, reading time and recall. *Journal of verbal learning and verbal behavior, 17*(1), February 1978, 13-28.

KIRBY, Katherine (1977). Structural ambiguity and sentence processing. Paper presented at the Language and Speech Conference, University of Melbourne, November 1977.

KIRBY, Katherine (1979). Semantic ambiguity and sentence processing. MSc thesis, Department of Psychology, University of Melbourne, 1979.

KLAPPHOLZ, A David and LOCKMAN, Abe David (1975). Contextual reference resolution. in: Diller 1975, microfiche 36, 4-25.

KLAPPHOLZ, A David and LOCKMAN, Abe David (1977). The use of dynamically extracted context for anaphoric reference resolution. Unpublished MS, Department of Electrical Engineering and Computer Science, Columbia University, New York, February 1977.

KUNO, Susumu (1975). Three perspectives in the functional approach to syntax. in: Robin E Grossman, L James San and Timothy J Vance (editors). *Papers from the parasession on functionalism*, Chicago Linguistic Society, 1975, 276-336.

LAKOFF, George (1968). Instrumental adverbs and the concept of deep structure. *Foundations of language, 4*, 1968, 4-29.

LAKOFF, George (1971). On generative semantics. [1] in: Danny D Steinberg and Leon A Jakobovits (editors) (1971). *Semantics: An interdisciplinary reader in philosophy, linguistics and psychology*. Cambridge University Press, 1971, 232-296. [2] an earlier version appeared in: *Papers from the fifth regional meeting*, Chicago Linguistic Society, 1969.

LAKOFF, George (1976). Pronouns and reference. [1] in: McCawley 1976, 275-335. [2] also published as: mimeo, Bloomington, Indiana: Indiana University

Linguistics Club, 1968.

LAKOFF, George and ROSS, John Robert (1972). A note on anaphoric islands and causatives. *Linguistic inquiry*, *3*(1), Summer 1972, 121-127.

LANGACKER, Ronald W (1969). On pronominalization and the chain of command. in: Reibel and Schane 1969, 160-186.

LEHRER, Adrienne (1975). Talking about wine. *Language*, *51*(4), December 1975, 901-923.

LI, Charles N (editor) (1975). *Subject and topic*. New York: Academic Press, 1975. [Some errata to this work were published in: *Lingua*, *43*(1), October 1977, page 97.]

LINSKY, Leonard (1963). [1] Reference and referents. in: Caton 1963, 74-89. [2] part of this work was published as: Hesperus and phosphorous. *Philosophical review*, *LXVIII*, 1959, 515-518.

LOCKMAN, Abe David (1978). Contextual reference resolution [1] PhD dissertation, Faculty of Pure Science, Columbia University, May 1978. [2] Technical report DCS-TR-70, Department of Computer Science, Rutgers University, 1978.

MACKWORTH, Alan Keith (1978). Vision research strategy: Black magic, metaphors, mechanisms, miniworlds and maps. in: Allen R Hanson and Edward M Riseman (editors). *Computer vision systems*. New York: Academic Press, 1978.

McCALLA, Gordon Irvine (1977). An approach to the organization of knowledge for the modelling of conversation. [1] PhD thesis, Department of Computer Science, University of British Columbia, June 1977. [2] abridged version published as: Technical report 78-4, Department of Computer Science, University of British Columbia, February 1978.

McCAWLEY, James D (1968). Lexical insertion in a transformational grammar without deep structure. *Papers from the fourth regional meeting*, Chicago Linguistic Society, April 1968, 71-80.

McCAWLEY, James D (editor) (1976). *Syntax and semantics 7: Notes from the linguistic underground*. New York: Academic Press, 1976.

McDONALD, David Daniel (1978a). A simultaniously [sic] procedural and declarative data structure and its use in natural language generation. *Proceedings of the second national conference*, Canadian Society for Computational Studies of Intelligence/Societe canadienne des etudes d'intelligence par ordinateur. Toronto, July 1978, 38-47.

McDONALD, David Daniel (1978b). Subsequent reference: syntactic and rhetorical constraints. in: Waltz 1978, 64-72.

MINSKY, Marvin Lee (editor) (1968). *Semantic information processing*. Cambridge, Massachusetts: MIT Press, 1968.

MINSKY, Marvin Lee (1975). A framework for representing knowledge. [1] in: Patrick Henry Winston (editor). *The psychology of computer vision*. McGraw-Hill, 1975, 211-280. [2] Memo 306, Artificial Intelligence Laborartory, Massachusetts Institute of Technology, June 1974. [3] a condensed version appears in: Schank and Nash-Webber 1975, 118-130. [4] version 3 also appears as: Frame-system theory. in: Philip Nicholas Johnson-Laird and Peter Cathcart Wason (editors). *Thinking: Readings in cognitive science*. Cambridge University Press, 1977, 355-376.

MORGAN, Jerry L (1968). Some strange aspects of *it*. *Papers from the fourth regional meeting*, Chicago Linguistic Society, April 1968, 81-93.

MORGAN, Jerry L (1978). Towards a rational model of discourse comprehension. in: Waltz 1978, 109-114.

NASH-WEBBER, Bonnie Lynn. *See also* Webber, Bonnie Lynn.

NASH-WEBBER, Bonnie Lynn (1976). Semantic interpretation revisited. Report 3335 (AI report 48), Bolt Beranek and Newman Inc, Cambridge, Massachusetts, July 1976.

NASH-WEBBER, Bonnie Lynn (1977). Anaphora: A cross-disciplinary survey. Technical report CSR-31, Center for the Study of Reading, University of Illinois at Urbana-Champaign, April 1977.

NASH-WEBBER, Bonnie Lynn and REITER, Raymond (1977). Anaphora and logical form: on formal meaning representations for natural language. [1] *Proceedings of the fifth international joint conference on artificial intelligence*. Cambridge, Massachusetts, August 1977, 121-131. [2] Technical report CSR-36, Center for the Study of Reading, University of Illinois at Urbana-Champaign, 1977.

NASH-WEBBER, Bonnie Lynn and SAG, Ivan A (1978). Under whose control? *Linguistic inquiry*, 9(1), Winter 1978, 138-141.

NELSON, Ruth (1978). The first literate computers? *Psychology today*, 11(10), March 1978, 72-80.

NORMAN, Donald A; RUMELHART, David E and the LNR Research Group (1975). *Explorations in cognition*. San Francisco: W H Freeman, 1975.

ORNE, Martin T (1962). On the social psychology of the psychological experiment: with particular reference to demand characteristics and their implications. *American psychologist*, 17(11), November 1962, 776-783.

ORTONY, Andrew (1978). Some psycholinguistic constraints on the construction and interpretation of definite descriptions. in: Waltz 1978, 73-78.

PARTEE, Barbara Hall (1978). Bound variables and other anaphors. in: Waltz 1978, 79-85.

PERRAULT, Charles Raymond and COHEN, Philip R (1977). Planning speech acts. AI memo 77-1, Department of Computer Science, University of Toronto, June 1977.

PETRICK, Stanley R (1976). On natural language based computer systems. [1] *IBM journal of research and development*, *20*(4), July 1976, 314-325. [2] in: Zampolli 1977, 313-340.

PHILLIPS, Brian (1975). Judging the coherency of discourse. in: Diller 1975, microfiche 35, 36-49.

PHILLIPS, Brian (1977). Discourse connectives. Technical report KSL-11, Knowledge Systems Laboratory, Department of Information Engineering, University of Illinois at Chicago Circle, March 1977.

PITKIN, Willis L Jr (1977a). Hierarchies and the discourse hierarchy. *College English*, *38*(7), March 1977, 648-659.

PITKIN, Willis L Jr (1977b). X/Y: Some basic strategies of discourse. *College English*, *38*(7), March 1977, 660-672.

POSTAL, Paul Martin (1969). Anaphoric islands. *Papers from the fifth regional meeting*, Chicago Linguistic Society, April 1969, 205-239.

POSTAL, Paul Martin (1976). Linguistic anarchy notes. in: McCawley 1976, 201-225.

REIBEL, David A and SCHANE, Sanford A (1969). *Modern studies in English: Readings in transformational grammar*. Englewood Cliffs, New Jersey: Prentice-Hall, 1969.

REICHMAN, Rachel (1978a). Conversational coherency. *Cognitive science*, *2*(4), October-December 1978, 283-327.

REICHMAN, Rachel (1978b). Conversational coherency. Technical report TR-17-78, [Department of ?], Harvard University, 1978.

RIEGER, Charles J III (1975). Conceptual memory and inference. in: Schank 1975, 157-288.

RIEGER, Charles J III (1978). The importance of multiple choice. [1] in: Waltz 1978, supplement. [2] Technical report 656, Department of Computer Science, University of Maryland, 1978.

ROBERTS, R Bruce and GOLDSTEIN, Ira P (1977a). The FRL primer. Memo 408, Artificial Intelligence Laboratory, Massachusetts Institute of Technology, July 1977.

ROBERTS, R Bruce and GOLDSTEIN, Ira P (1977b). The FRL manual. Memo 409, Artificial Intelligence Laboratory, Massachusetts Institute of Technology, September 1977.

ROSENBERG, Steven T (1976). Discourse structure. Working paper 130, Artificial Intelligence Laboratory, Massachusetts Institute of Technology, 17 August 1976.

ROSENBERG, Steven T (1977). Frame-based text processing. Memo 431, Artificial Intelligence Laboratory, Massachusetts Institute of Technology, November 1977.

ROSS, John Robert (1969). On the cyclic nature of English pronominalization. [1] in: Reibel and Schane 1969, 187-200. [2] in: *To honor Roman Jakobson*. The Hague: Mouton, 1967, volume II, 1669-1682.

RUSSELL, Bertrand (1905). On denoting. [1] *Mind, XIV* (number 56), October 1905, 479-493. [2] in: Bertrand Russell. *Logic and knowledge: Essays 1901-1950* (edited by Robert Charles Marsh). London: Allen and Unwin, 1956. [3] in: Herbert Feigl and Wilfrid Sellars (editors). *Readings in philosophical analysis*. New York: Appleton-Century-Crofts, 1949.

SAG, Ivan A (1976). Deletion and logical form. [1] PhD thesis, Department of Foreign Literatures and Linguistics, Massachusetts Institute of Technology, 1976. [2] published in the series: Outstanding dissertations in linguistics, New York: 'Garland Publishing, 1980.

SCHACHTER, Paul (1977). Does she or doesn't she? *Linguistic inquiry, 8*(4), Fall 1977, 763-767.

SCHANK, Roger Carl (1973). Identification of conceptualizations underlying natural language. in: Schank and Colby 1973, 187-247.

SCHANK, Roger Carl (1975). *Conceptual information processing*. Amsterdam: North-Holland, 1975.

SCHANK, Roger Carl and ABELSON, Robert P (1975). Scripts, plans and knowledge. *Advance papers of the fourth international joint conference on artificial intelligence*. Tblisi, USSR, 151-157.

SCHANK, Roger Carl and ABELSON, Robert P (1977). *Scripts, plans, goals and understanding: An enquiry into human knowledge structures*. Hillsdale, New Jersey: Lawrence Erlbaum Associates, 1977.

SCHANK, Roger Carl and COLBY, Kenneth Mark (1973). *Computer models of thought and language*. San Francisco: W H Freeman, 1973.

SCHANK, Roger Carl; GOLDMAN, Neil Murray; RIEGER, Charles J III and RIESBECK, Christopher Kevin (1975). Inference and paraphrase by computer. *Journal of the Association for Computing Machinery, 22*(3), July 1975, 309-328.

SCHANK, Roger Carl and NASH-WEBBER, Bonnie Lynn (1975). *Theoretical issues in natural language processing: An inter-disciplinary workshop*. Cambridge, Massachusetts: Association for Computational Linguistics, June 1975.

SCHANK, Roger Carl and the Yale AI Project (1975). SAM — A story understander. Research report 43, Department of Computer Science, Yale University, 1975.

SGALL, Petr; HAJIČOVÁ, Eva and BENEŠOVÁ, Eva (1973). *Topic, focus and generative semantics*. Kronberg Taunus: Scriptor Verlag, 1973.

SHANNON, Claude E and WEAVER, Warren (1949). *The mathematical theory of communication*. Urbana: University of Illinois Press, 1949.

SIDNER, Candace Lee. *see also* Bullwinkle, Candace Lee.

SIDNER, Candace Lee (1978a). A progress report on the discourse and reference components of PAL. [1] in: *Proceedings of the second national conference*, Canadian Society for Computational Studies of Intelligence/Societe canadienne des etudes d'intelligence par ordinateur. Toronto, July 1978, 206-213. [2] Memo 468, Artificial Intelligence Laboratory, Massachusetts Institute of Technology, 1978.

SIDNER, Candace Lee (1978b). The use of focus as a tool for the disambiguation of definite noun phrases. in: Waltz 1978, 86-95.

SIDNER, Candace Lee (1979). Towards a computational theory of definite anaphora comprehension in English discourse. [1] PhD thesis, Department of Electrical Engineering and Computer Science, Massachusetts Institute of Technology, 16 May 1979. [2] revised version: Technical Report 537, Artificial Intelligence Laboratory, Massachusetts Institute of Technology, June 1979.

SONDHEIMER, Norman K (1977a). Towards a combined representation for spatial and temporal knowledge. *Proceedings of the fifth international joint conference on artificial intelligence*. Cambridge, Massachusetts, August 1977, 281-282.

SONDHEIMER, Norman K (1977b). Spatial reference and semantic nets. *American journal of computational linguistics*, microfiche 71, 1977.

SPENCER, N J (1973). Differences between linguists and non-linguists in intuitions of grammaticality-acceptability. *Journal of psycholinguistic research*, *2*(2), April 1973, 83-98.

SPRINGSTON, F (1976). Verb-derived constraints in the comprehension of anaphoric pronouns. Paper presented at the Eastern Psychological Association, 1976.

STRAWSON, Peter Frederick (1950). On referring. [1] *Mind, LIX* (number 235), July 1950, 320-344. [2] in: Caton 1963. [3] in: Antony Flew (editor). *Essays on conceptual analysis*. London: MacMillan, 1956, 21-52.

TAYLOR, Brock Harold (1975). A case-driven parser. Unpublished MSc thesis, Department of Computer Science, University of British Columbia, May 1975.

TAYLOR, Brock Harold and ROSENBERG, Richard Stuart (1975). A case-driven parser for natural language. [1] *American journal of computational linguistics*, microfiche 31, 1975. [2] also published as: Technical report 75-5, Department of Computer Science, University of British Columbia, October 1975.

THOMAS, Andrew L (1979). Ellipsis: The interplay of sentence structure and context. *Lingua*, *47*(1), January 1979, 43-68.

WALKER, Donald E (editor) (1976). Speech understanding research. SRI Project 4762, Final technical report, SRI International, October 1976.

WALKER, Donald E (editor) (1978). *Understanding spoken language*. (The computer science library, Artificial intelligence series *5*), New York: North-Holland, 1978.

WALTZ, David L (editor) (1978). *TINLAP-2: Theoretical issues in natural language processing-2*. University of Illinois at Urbana-Champaign, 25-27 July 1978.

WASOW, Thomas Alexander (1975). Anaphoric pronouns and bound variables. *Language*, *51*(2), June 1975, 368-383.

WATT, William C (1968). Habitability. *American documentation* [now *Journal of the American Society for Information Science*], *19*(3), July 1968, 338-351.

WATT, William C (1973). Late lexicalizations. in: Kaarlo Jaako Juhani Hintikka, Julius Matthew Emil Moravcsik and Patrick Colonel Suppes (editors). *Approaches to natural language: Proceedings of the 1970 Stanford workshop on grammar and semantics*. Dordrecht: Reidel, 1973.

WATT, William C (1975). The indiscreteness with which impenetrables are penetrated. *Lingua*, *37*, 1975, 95-128.

WEBBER, Bonnie Lynn. *see also* Nash-Webber, Bonnie Lynn.

WEBBER, Bonnie Lynn (1978a). A formal approach to discourse anaphora. [1] Report 3761, Bolt Beranek and Newman Inc, May 1978. [2] PhD thesis, Harvard University, 1978. [3] published in the series: Outstanding dissertations in linguistics, New York: Garland Publishing, 1979.

WEBBER, Bonnie Lynn (1978b). Description formation and discourse model synthesis. in: Waltz 1978, 42-50.

WEIZENBAUM, Joseph (1976). *Computer power and human reason: From judgment to calculation*. San Francisco: W H Freeman, 1976.

WHITLEY, M Stanley (1978). Person and number in the use of *we*, *you*, and *they*. *American speech*, *53*(1), Spring 1978, 18-39.

WILKS, Yorick Alexander (1971). Decidability and natural language. *Mind*, *LXXX* (number 320), October 1971, 497-520.

WILKS, Yorick Alexander (1973a). An artificial intelligence approach to machine translation. in: Schank and Colby 1973, 114-151.

WILKS, Yorick Alexander (1973b). Preference semantics. [1] Stanford Artificial Intelligence Laboratory memo AIM-206/Stanford University Computer Science report CS-337, July 1973. [2] also published in: Edward Louis Keenan III (editor). *Formal semantics of natural language*. Cambridge University Press, 1975, 329-348.

WILKS, Yorick Alexander (1975a). An intelligent analyzer and understander of English. *Communications of the ACM*, *18*(5), May 1975, 264-274.

WILKS, Yorick Alexander (1975b). A preferential pattern-seeking semantics for natural language inference. *Artificial intelligence*, *6*, 1975, 53-74.

WILKS, Yorick Alexander (1975c). Methodology in AI and natural language. [1] in: Schank and Nash-Webber 1975, 144-147. [2] a revised version appears in: Yorick Alexander Wilks. Seven theses on artificial intelligence and natural language. Working paper 17, Institute for Semantic and Cognitive Studies, Geneva, 1975, 3-12. [3] another revised version appears as part of: Yorick Alexander Wilks. Methodological questions about artificial intelligence: Approaches to understanding natural language. *Journal of pragmatics*, *1*(1), April 1977, 69-84.

WINOGRAD, Terry (1971). Procedures as a representation of data in a computer program for understanding natural language. Technical report 17, Artificial Intelligence Laboratory, Massachusetts Institute of Technology, February 1971.

WINOGRAD, Terry (1972). *Understanding natural language*. [1] New York: Academic Press, 1972. [2] Edinburgh University Press, 1972. [3] also published in: *Cognitive psychology*, *3*(1), 1972, 1-191.

WINSTON, Patrick Henry (1977). [1] *Artificial Intelligence*. Reading, Massachusetts: Addison-Wesley, 1977. [2] An earlier version was circulated as: *Notes on computer intelligence*, May 1976.

WOODS, William A (1968). Procedural semantics for a question-answering machine. *AFIPS conference proceedings*, *33*, FJCC 1968, 457-471.

WOODS, William A (1970). Transition network grammars for natural language analysis. *Communications of the ACM*, *13*(10), October 1970, 591-606.

WOODS, William A (1977). Lunar rocks in natural English: Explorations in natural language question answering. in: Zampolli 1977, 521-569.

WOODS, William A; KAPLAN, Ronald M and NASH-WEBBER, Bonnie Lynn (1972). The Lunar Science Natural Language Information System: Final report. Report 2378, Bolt Beranek and Newman Inc, Cambridge, Massachusetts, June 1972.

ZAMPOLLI, Antonio (1977). *Linguistic structures processing*. (= Fundamental studies in computer science 5). Amsterdam: North-Holland, 1977.

INDEX OF NAMES

SUBJECT INDEX

77: G. V. Bochmann, Architecture of Distributed Computer
tems. VIII, 238 pages. 1979.

78: M. Gordon, R. Milner and C. Wadsworth, Edinburgh LCF.
159 pages. 1979.

79: Language Design and Programming Methodology. Pro-
dings, 1979. Edited by J. Tobias. IX, 255 pages. 1980.

80: Pictorial Information Systems. Edited by S. K. Chang and
. Fu. IX, 445 pages. 1980.

81: Data Base Techniques for Pictorial Applications. Proceed-
, 1979. Edited by A. Blaser. XI, 599 pages. 1980.

82: J. G. Sanderson, A Relational Theory of Computing. VI,
pages. 1980.

83: International Symposium Programming. Proceedings, 1980.
ed by B. Robinet. VII, 341 pages. 1980.

84: Net Theory and Applications. Proceedings, 1979. Edited
J. Brauer. XIII, 537 Seiten. 1980.

35: Automata, Languages and Programming. Proceedings,1980.
ed by J. de Bakker and J. van Leeuwen. VIII, 671 pages. 1980.

86: Abstract Software Specifications. Proceedings,1979. Edited
, Bjørner. XIII, 567 pages. 1980

87: 5th Conference on Automated Deduction. Proceedings,
. Edited by W. Bibel and R. Kowalski. VII, 385 pages. 1980.

88: Mathematical Foundations of Computer Science 1980.
eedings, 1980. Edited by P. Dembiński. VIII, 723 pages. 1980.

89: Computer Aided Design - Modelling, Systems Engineering,
-Systems. Proceedings, 1980. Edited by J. Encarnacao. XIV,
pages. 1980.

90: D. M. Sandford, Using Sophisticated Models in Reso-
n Theorem Proving.
39 pages. 1980

91: D. Wood, Grammar and L Forms: An Introduction. IX, 314
es. 1980.

92: R. Milner, A Calculus of Communication Systems. VI, 171
es. 1980.

93: A. Nijholt, Context-Free Grammars: Covers, Normal Forms,
Parsing. VII, 253 pages. 1980.

94: Semantics-Directed Compiler Generation. Proceedings,
. Edited by N. D. Jones. V, 489 pages. 1980.

95: Ch. D. Marlin, Coroutines. XII, 246 pages. 1980.

96: J. L. Peterson, Computer Programs for Spelling Correction:
3 pages. 1980.

97: S. Osaki and T. Nishio, Reliability Evaluation of Some Fault-
ant Computer Architectures. VI, 129 pages. 1980.

98: Towards a Formal Description of Ada. Edited by D. Bjørner
D. N. Oest. XIV, 630 pages. 1980.

99: I. Guessarian, Algebraic Semantics. XI, 158 pages. 1981.

00: Graphtheoretic Concepts in Computer Science. Edited by
Itemeier. X, 403 pages. 1981.

01: A. Thayse, Boolean Calculus of Differences. VII, 144 pages.

02: J. H. Davenport, On the Integration of Algebraic Functions.
7 pages. 1981.

03: H. Ledgard, A. Singer, J. Whiteside, Directions in Human
rs of Interactive Systems. VI, 190 pages. 1981.

04: Theoretical Computer Science. Ed. by P. Deussen. VII,
ages. 1981.

05: B. W. Lampson, M. Paul, H. J. Siegert, Distributed Systems –
tecture and Implementation. XIII, 510 pages. 1981.

06: The Programming Language Ada. Reference Manual. X,
ages. 1981.

Vol. 107: International Colloquium on Formalization of Programming
Concepts. Proceedings. Edited by J. Diaz and I. Ramos. VII, 478
pages. 1981.

Vol. 108: Graph Theory and Algorithms. Edited by N. Saito and
T. Nishizeki. VI, 216 pages. 1981.

Vol. 109: Digital Image Processing Systems. Edited by L. Bolc and
Zenon Kulpa. V, 353 pages. 1981.

Vol. 110: W. Dehning, H. Essig, S. Maass, The Adaptation of Virtual
Man-Computer Interfaces to User Requirements in Dialogs. X, 142
pages. 1981.

Vol. 111: CONPAR 81. Edited by W. Händler. XI, 508 pages. 1981.

Vol. 112: CAAP '81. Proceedings. Edited by G. Astesiano and C. Böhm.
VI, 364 pages. 1981.

Vol. 113: E.-E. Doberkat, Stochastic Automata: Stability, Nondeter-
minism, and Prediction. IX, 135 pages. 1981.

Vol. 114: B. Liskov, CLU, Reference Manual. VIII, 190 pages. 1981.

Vol. 115: Automata, Languages and Programming. Edited by S. Even
and O. Kariv. VIII, 552 pages. 1981.

Vol. 116: M. A. Casanova, The Concurrency Control Problem for
Database Systems. VII, 175 pages. 1981.

Vol. 117: Fundamentals of Computation Theory. Proceedings, 1981.
Edited by F. Gécseg. XI, 471 pages. 1981.

Vol. 118: Mathematical Foundations of Computer Science 1981.
Proceedings, 1981. Edited by J. Gruska and M. Chytil. XI, 589 pages.
1981.

Vol. 119: G. Hirst, Anaphora in Natural Language Understanding:
A Survey. XIII, 128 pages. 1981.

This series reports new developments in computer science research a
teaching – quickly, informally and at a high level. The type of matei
considered for publication includes:

1. Preliminary drafts of original papers and monographs
2. Lectures on a new field or presentations of a new angle in a classi
   field
3. Seminar work-outs
4. Reports of meetings, provided they are
   a) of exceptional interest and
   b) devoted to a single topic.

Texts which are out of print but still in demand may also be consider
if they fall within these categories.

The timeliness of a manuscript is more important than its form, whi
may be unfinished or tentative. Thus, in some instances, proofs may
merely outlined and results presented which have been or will la
be published elsewhere. If possible, a subject index should be includ
Publication of Lecture Notes is intended as a service to the internatio
computer science community, in that a commercial publisher, Spring
Verlag, can offer a wide distribution of documents which would oth
wise have a restricted readership. Once published and copyrighte
they can be documented in the scientific literature.

Manuscripts

Manuscripts should be no less than 100 and preferably no more than 500 pages in length.
They are reproduced by a photographic process and therefore must be typed with extreme care. Sym
not on the typewriter should be inserted by hand in indelible black ink. Corrections to the types
should be made by pasting in the new text or painting out errors with white correction fluid. Authors rec
75 free copies and are free to use the material in other publications. The typescript is reduced sligh
size during reproduction; best results will not be obtained unless the text on any one page is kept w
the overall limit of 18 x 26.5 cm (7 x 10½ inches). On request, the publisher will supply special paper
the typing area outlined.
Manuscripts should be sent to Prof. G. Goos, Institut für Informatik, Universität Karlsruhe, Zirkel 2, 7500 K
ruhe/Germany, Prof. J. Hartmanis, Cornell University, Dept. of Computer-Science, Ithaca, NY/USA 14
or directly to Springer-Verlag Heidelberg.

Springer-Verlag, Heidelberger Platz 3, D-1000 Berlin 33
Springer-Verlag, Neuenheimer Landstraße 28–30, D-6900 Heidelberg 1
Springer-Verlag, 175 Fifth Avenue, New York, NY 10010/USA

ISBN 3-540-10858-0
ISBN 0-387-10858-0